DISCLAIMER

Special Acknowledgments
Mirror of Ezred Web Site, John Neilan - Claire Neilan
Collaboration - Kristen Sutton, Hilton Head Island, SC
Joanne Dunn / Dawn Byrd - Consulting Editors
Sheila Clark Mouser - Faithful Support

Library of Congress Cataloging in Publication Data
Entered into an Act of Congress - L C Control Number
2001 131094

HP Publishing USA
A division of HP Publications, LTD..
P. . Box 21455
Hilton Head Island, SC 29925

ISBN 1 - 929771 - 05 - 3

Author - David B. Mouser

Illustrated by Ralph Sutton

Printed and bound in the United States of America

First Edition
10 9 8 7 6 5 4 3 2 1

Harry Potter's Muggles' Guide to Magic

J. K. Rowling, a single mother on welfare, wrote *The Sorcerer's Stone* on scraps of paper at a local café in England. Encouraged by her college teachers and friends, she undertook writing her first book, and with the help of a university grant and a little luck, Rowling was able to finish her first manuscript and publish a small quantity of books. It soon became a huge success and topped the best seller's list in countries all over the world.

The Sorcerer's Stone, the first book in a series of seven, begins our journey into the world of magic and in particular the adolescent world of Harry Potter. Harry is an 11 year orphan boy living with relatives just outside London, England. He finds out he is a very special person, the son of a wizard family. He is famous in the magical community of wizards for having caused the villain, Lord Voldemort, a dark wizard who was taking over the world, to disappear. Everyone in this magical community knows the name Harry Potter and marvels at his deed, yet neither he nor anyone else knows how he did it.

He was not more than a year old when Lord Voldemort attempted to kill him, killing his parents who tried to stand in his way. Harry survived because a powerful protection charm was placed upon him by his dying mother. The charm caused Voldemort's magical attack to backfire, reducing him to a shadowy vapor and allowing him to exist only when sharing another's body. Harry received a lightning bolt scar on his forehead from the experience and unknowingly absorbed some of Voldemort's powers.

Thus Harry has become Voldemort's most sought after target for revenge, yet ironically, Voldemort needs Harry in order to restore his original powers. Harry spends the first 10 years of his life growing up with his Muggle (non 'wizarding') relatives. Upon reaching age 11, however, Harry's world changes abruptly. He receives a mysterious letter informing him that he has been accepted at Hogwarts School for Witchcraft and Wizardry.

Harry Potter's Muggles' Guide to Magic

Harry Potter is to journey to Hogwarts, where he is to learn how to become a wizard. He will attend each year for 7 years. At Hogwarts, Harry becomes a star athlete in the wizarding sport of Quidditch (a lightning fast game played in the air on broomsticks; the object being to catch a golden snitch). Each book in the series tells of one year's adventures at Hogwarts from the time he is a 1st year student until his graduation in his 7th year.

Constant throughout the series is the villain, Lord Voldemort, also frequently referred to as 'he who must not be named'. Harry must face serious threats and sinister actions as Lord Voldemort plots at every turn to kill him and return to power.

In addition to Harry Potter and Lord Voldemort, two other main characters are developed throughout the series. Herimone Granger and Ron Weasley are fellow students at Hogwarts. Herimone, Ron, and Harry become the "three musketeers" as they experience the adventure, mystery, and suspense of the magical world that exists all around us but which cannot be seen by Muggles (the non magical people of the world).

In his first year at Hogwarts, Harry learns about the mysterious sorcerer's stone. The sorcerer's stone has 2 powers: it turns things to gold, and it can be used to create an elixir of life. Albert Dumbledore, the headmaster, and his best friend Nicolas Flamel are the only two alive who know how to make a sorcerer's stone, but they choose not to because they fear that Voldemort may acquire one and use it to return to power.

Also during this first year, Harry learns about his archenemy, the Dark Wizard Lord Voldemort, whose obsession with killing Harry drives everything he does.

The basic theme throughout the books is, of course, Good vs. Evil. Harry Potter represents the child in all of us: sensitive, adventuresome, and filled with an insatiable desire to find out "what lies on the other side of the mountain". His world is very interesting, as magic has always fascinated mankind.

Harry Potter's Muggles' Guide to Magic

J. K. Rowling weaves a tight web of interlocking characters, story themes and mysteries. Clues and information are subtly revealed throughout each book enabling the reader to solve each mystery. These elements are wonderfully woven into the final chapters, not only revealing the solution to each mystery but also providing information that is essential to the further adventures of Harry Potter.

Throughout each book there are caches of easily overlooked and casually exposed information that will be essential to the development of other episodes and will provide additional clues to the future mysteries. As an example, could Harry Potter be the true heir of Godric Gryffindor? When he first purchases his wand in Ollivander's Wand Shop (in The Sorcerer's Stone), red and gold sparks shoot out of it. Red and gold are the colors of Gryffindor House at Hogwarts. Professor McGonagall, Deputy Head Mistress at Hogwarts, mentions in the prologue to Book 1, that Harry's parents lived in Godric Hollow (Named after Godric Gryffindor?). In The Chamber of Secrets, after Harry pulls Godric Gryffindor's sword out of the Sorting Hat, Professor Dumbledore, Head Master at Hogwarts, tells Harry that "Only a true Griffindor could have pulled it out!" Throughout the first four books we do not know if Harry is the true son of Lilly and James Potter, his "parents" who were killed by Voldemort, nor do we know for sure why Voldemort attempted to kill Harry. However, we do know that Voldemort is the heir of Salazar Slytherin, a wizard who lived in the same age of Gryffindor and later became his bitter adversary. This and many other such examples show that the Harry Potter books are not only individual stories complete within each book but also a large, complex mystery made up of 7 different puzzles which will come together in the final, 7th, book.

The Illustrated *Harry Potter's Muggle Guide to Magic* is your guide to understanding the world of Harry Potter. It includes a synopsis of each book, a muggles' guide for detail information and page reference, a complete glossary of people, places and things and wonderful illustrations by Ralph Sutton of Hilton Head Island, SC.

Harry Potter's Muggles' Guide to Magic

The glossary is divided into the following sections to provide quick reference to the reader:

Characters
Charms, Spells, Potions, Curses
Creatures
General Glossary
Ghosts
Places
Wizards
Wizardu Books

Your Muggle's guide to Magic is your "pocket guide" to Harry Potter's world. It will provide you with important information and reference material, enabling you to better understand each book. The Harry Potter books are wonderfully simple to read and yet they contain mountains of information and clues that the reader cannot possibly digest with just one reading. Many people are reading the books for the third and forth time to assimilate all of the stories and to thoroughly understand each mystery and adventure.

The reader will note that every care is taken not to reveal the mysteries, the adventures and the conclusion of each book, providing only the situations and highlights with the referencing page numbers. This allows you to re-visit that particular portion or chapter in the book, thus again providing further enjoyment, refreshing your memory and further explaining important facts and clues that are extremely important as you read each sequel story.

The illustrations are an important "camera" into Harry Potter's world. The movie series by Warner Brothers is the screen plays version of Harry's World. The Illustrated Harry Potter's Muggles Guide to Magic Illustrations are developed from the context of each page and presented in this publication to preserve in book form what a movie cannot accomplish.

INTRODUCTION
Harry Potter's Muggles' Guide to Magic

A picture can offer the individual a window into that thought and place. A movie is fast moving and each frame takes you where it wants without time for you to "imagine". In summary, it imagines for you - an illustration invites you to imagine for yourself . . . and each time you visit an illustration, you can imagine something different!!

You will find this guide invaluable for reference, before, during and after the reading of each and every book. It is truly your "Muggles Guide to Magic" and will provide you with a greater understanding of the clues and mysteries revealed in each Harry Potter book.

NOW . . . PREPARE YOURSELF
TO ENTER
HOGWARTS
AND PUT ON THE SORTING HAT

1st Year Students' Required School Supplies

Uniform

First-year students will require:

1. Three sets of plain work robes (black)
2. One plain pointed hate (black) for day wear
3. One pair of protective gloves (dragon hide or similar)
4. One winter cloak (black, silver fastenings)

Please note that all pupils' clothes should carry name tags

Course Books

All students should have a copy of each of the following:

The Standard Book of Spells (Grade 1)
    By Miranda Goshawk
A History of Magic by
    Bathilda Bagshot
Magical Theory by
    Adalbert Waffling
*A Beginners' Guide to
    Transfiguration* by
    Emeric Switch
*One Thousand Magical Herbs and
    Fungi* by Phyllida Spore

Magical Drafts and Potions
by Arsenius Jigger

Fantastic Beasts and Where To Find Them
by Newt Scamander

The Dark Forces: A Guide to Self-Protection
by Quentin Trimble

OTHER EQUIPMENT

1 Wand
    1 Cauldron (pewter, standard size 2)
    1 set glass or crystal phials
    1 telescope
    1 set brass scales

Students may also bring an owl OR a cat OR a toad

PARENTS ARE REMINDED THAT FIRST YEARS ARE NOT ALLOWED THEIR OWN BROOMSTICKS

The Hogwarts School of Witchcraft and Wizardry was founded over a thousand years ago. The precise date is unknown, even by the four greatest wizards of the age. The school is housed in a castle surrounded by The Forbidden Forest. The forest and adjacent lake are filled with numerous magical creatures. The Village of Hogsmeade, whose inhabitants are all wizards and witches, is across the lake where the Hogwarts Express stops each year bringing the students to school.

The four great wizards (Hufflepuff, Slytherin, Gryffindor and Ravenclaw) built the castle far from prying Muggle eyes, for it was during an age when magic was feared by common people, and when witches and wizards suffered much persecution.

Hogwarts is protected by a special magical environment and by spells placed upon it by the Great Wizards. Ghosts wander through the many hidden chambers, and the huge towers provide residence for the attending students. The Great Hall doubles as the dining chamber where most of the school activities are held. In the Great Hall, the magical ceiling changes with the sky outside and is alive with moving objects. Hogwarts, located in the mountains of Scotland, is protected from Muggles' eyes by magical spells, appearing to them as an old ruin. The magic of the castle is constantly apparent, as the rooms, floors, and dungeons change locations frequently.

Harry Potter

Harry Potter, until his 11th birthday, believed he was an ordinary child. In addition to the normal attitude of a youth about to become a teenager, he has an eager, inquisitive mind. Though he is humble, he is also independent, confident, and even assertive in his general behavior.

An orphan, Harry yearns constantly to identify with his parents, Lilly and James Potter, who died at the hand of Lord Voldemort when Harry was only one year old. He is also drawn to Albus Dumbledore, the headmaster of his school, as a fatherly figure, and he comes to rely upon Sirius Black, his godfather, as an anchor in life.

His happiness is centered around Hogwarts School of Witchcraft and Wizardry. He had led a miserable life with his Aunt and Uncle who regarded him as a liability since they are Muggles (non wizards) and resent anyone who is involved in magic.

Harry is unperturbed by the constant threat of Lord Voldemort's plan to return and kill him but is ever vigilant to the threat. His character values are centered around "fair play": honesty, selflessness, and bravery. As Harry grows older he begins to mature in these qualities. Harry exhibits the natural ability to combat the evil forces that are ever present in J. K. Rowling's novels.

Hermione Granger

Hermione, a bushy haired, buck toothed 11 year old girl becomes Harry's trusted friend and confidante. A studious pupil, Hermione's character is somewhat subdued. She is ever watchful for Harry's good health and always there to help out when needed. Her character values are identical to Harry's but from the standpoint of the female gender. Hermione plays a supportive role in all of Harry's adventures.

Albus Dumbledore

Dumbledore is headmaster of Hogwarts School of Witchcraft and Wizardry. He is possibly the most interesting character and certainly the least developed in the first 4 initial books. Dumbledore is the only wizard that Voldemort avoids because of his magical powers. He represents the old wizard community. Dumbledore always allows Harry to investigate the mysteries, while watching quietly over Harry and then appearing in the conclusion to provide the assistance needed. He also becomes the moderator of the conclusion in each book providing an intelligent overview of what has happened, yet remaining humble in his explanations. He is cool under fire and remains an anchor to Hogwarts in addition to being the underlying strength in the Wizarding world.

Ron Weasley

Ron, also 11 years old, is the third member of the trio of friends. Ron is one of the six Weasley children and is ready to support Harry in almost any situation. His desire to be important stems from being over-shadowed by Harry's fame in the wizarding world and from his need for individuality. Likable and mischievous, Ron is Harry's constant companion in all of the adventures. He provides the reader with a constant subtle criticism of Harry, yet he is always ready to defend Harry against The Dark Lord (Lord Voldemort). He exhibits trustworthy values and loyalty which are the hallmark values of friendship.

Ron's character values continue to build in each book. He is a solid supporting character always providing Harry with friendship and support through out each adventure. Ron also represents a stable platform for the reader to understand what it is like to be raised in a 100% wizarding family.

Rubius Hagrid

A very lovable, over sized and genuinely simple grounds keeper Rubius Hagrid provides comic relief through his desire to keep dangerous magical creatures as pets. He is trustworthy, loyal and friendly. Second only to Sirius Black, Hagrid is Harry's protector and often provides important information in each adventure. Hagrid lives at Hogwarts on the edge of the Forbidden Forest and was once a pupil at Hogwarts. He is trusted by Dumbledore, yet often lacks common sense and represents simplicity, which is present in all our lives but which is frequently overlooked as a true virtue.

Professor McGonagall

Professor McGonagall is the deputy headmistress of Hogwarts and is the stabilizing force providing discipline and order at the school. She exhibits stability and is loyal to Dumbledore and the principles of Witchcraft. McGonagall provides the cohesive force that binds the school together and is involved in school activities as an organizer and authority. In contrast, Dumbledore is often distant and only appears at the annual school opening and at times of intense mystery and at story conclusions.

Sirius Black

Strong willed and mentally focused, Sirius Black is a very solid character who is Harry's godfather and only remaining family member. Falsely accused of terrible crimes, Sirius has spent time in Azkaban Prison. He is an anamagnis, having the ability to transform into an animal at will in order to disguise himself as he flees from the Dementors who pursue him. Sirius watches over Harry and is a source for information about Voldemort's past, about the Death Eaters (Voldemort's followers) and about Harry's parents.

Lord Voldemort
(The Dark Lord)
a.k.a.
"He Who Must Not Be Named")

Voldemort is the 'king' of villains. He is cunning, deceitful and represents everything that is evil in the Good vs. Evil theme of each novel. Voldemort is constantly seeking revenge on Harry. His attempt to kill Harry as a baby has resulted in his losing his physical body and much of his magical powers. He believes that Harry's death will re-establish his respect in the Dark Wizard world of Death Eaters (his loyal supporters). Voldemort's main character weakness is his constant need to seek revenge against Harry. It even interferes with his return to power. As evidenced by his loyal follower Wormtail in Book 4, The Goblet of Fire, Voldemort could regain his power by other means, but his desire for revenge blinds him to any other solutions.

Draco Malfoy

Draco, the son of Lucius Malfoy, who practices the Dark Arts, constantly antagonizes Harry. Draco is the bully of the school, always tormenting others and especially Harry. Cowardly, dishonest, untrustworthy, deceitful and jealous of Harry and his friends, Draco is a constant thorn in Harry's side at Hogwarts. His character appears destined to be a main evil rival to Harry. Draco is Harry's constant and ever present enemy, just as Voldemort is his constant and seldom seen enemy. Draco may well be the heir to Voldemort's evil ways.

The Sorcerer's Stone is the first book in the Harry Potter series. Harry Potter, an 11 year old boy, has lived a miserable life with his aunt and uncle, the Dursleys, after his parents' death. Harry is forced to live in a spider filled cupboard under the Dursleys stairs for 10 years, but upon his eleventh birthday everything is about to change.

A mysterious letter inviting him to attend the Hogwarts School for Witchcraft and Wizardry arrives by Owl Post. Harry is amazed to learn the truth about his parents' death - they were wizards of the highest order - and that he himself is destined to become a wizard too.

The transition from Harry's mundane existence to the world of witchcraft, wizards, and fantasy provides a wonderful platform for the reader to leave the real world and experience the magical realm through the eyes of Harry Potter. This reader involvement is one of the essential elements of the success of the Harry Potter Books.

On his way to Hogwarts, Harry meets Ron Weasley and Hermione Granger, two fellow students who are to become his best friends. At Hogwarts he finds that he has a natural talent to play Quidditch. Quidditch is an aerial game played on broomsticks involving lightning speed and agility. As the school year progresses he becomes involved in a life-threatening struggle against the forces that killed his parents and learns that Lord Voldemort, the dark wizard, is responsible for his parents' deaths. Voldemort is trying to kill him in order to regain his full powers as a dark wizard.

The classic struggle of Good vs. Evil is the main theme throughout all of the Harry Potter books. In The Sorcerer's Stone, Harry and his friends Ron and Hermione will face this classic struggle as they begin their education at Hogwarts.

Each story unfolds a puzzle which the reader, along with Harry and his friends, must try to solve. They must do it alone without any outside help against all odds, without any of the adult wizards to help until the last few pages of each book. Harry's struggle against the dark powers of a mighty wizard provides us with a David and Goliath theme in the world of magic. Harry champions the theme of good and conquers evil in a suspense-filled conclusion with all the excitement, drama and conflict that will provide the reader with a conclusion not identified until the end.

The professors' and characters' names are actually names of herbs and plants. The authors of the Hogwarts textbooks are riddles and puns, and many of the creatures and places are developed from ancient mythology.

The Sorcerer's Stone is Harry's first adventure, and in it we learn that there is a magical and "legendary substance" created by a colleague and good friend of the headmaster of the wizard's school, Professor Dumbledore. It is called the Sorcerer's Stone or, in J. K. Rowling's English editions, the Philosopher's Stone. It can transform any metal into gold and it can be used to produce the "Elixir of Life, a potion which prolongs life indefinitely. The sorcerer's stone has been hidden in Hogwarts castle for safe keeping, but Lord Voldemort is attempting to capture it in order to return to power. Throughout the book, Harry finds himself in a desperate struggle to find the stone and to save himself from the Dark Lord's attempt to use the stone in order to regain power and destroy Harry.

The hiding place of the Sorcerer's Stone is revealed to be a place both thoroughly disguised yet fully exposed at all times.

The Sorcerer's Stone symbolizes mans' eternal desire for wealth and longevity, but it is clear that love is more important than money or life itself. It was pure love that moved Harry's mother to sacrifice her own life in an attempt to save his, and it was that love which provided the charm which reflected Voldemort's attack spell, destroying him. To be loved so deeply will always provide some protection against evil. Thus, Harry's greatest protection as he grows up is the love that was given to him by his mother.

The first chapter, "The Boy Who Lived", describes the two worlds of reality and fantasy that exist in London, England. Strange things are happening as we are introduced to the Dursleys. (Harry's Aunt Petunia, Uncle Vernon and their spoiled son Dudley) (Page 1,2,3,4,5,6,7)

Albus Dumbledore is introduced for the first time. (Page 8,9)

Lord Voldemort, also known as "he who must not be named" is introduced as the Villain. (Page 11,12)

Harry Potter arrives at #4 Privet Drive carried by Hagrid on Sirius Black's flying magical motorcycle at age 1. (Page 14)

Professor Dumbledore places Harry on the door step at the Dursleys (Page 16)

Ten years pass - Harry and Dudley Dursley visit the zoo where Harry finds out he can talk to snakes. (Page 27)

Harry is about to turn 11 years old when strange letters begin to arrive at #4 Privet Drive. Uncle Vernon keeps them from Harry because they are addressed to "Harry" in "The Cupboard Under The Stairs", causing concern that Harry's living conditions may cause trouble. More and more letters arrive and Uncle Vernon takes the entire family and escapes to Cokeworth where the letters continue to follow them. (Page 41,42)

Hagrid appears on Harry's birthday in Cokeworth where Uncle Vernon believes he has hidden his family. She brings Harry a birthday present (sticky chocolate cake). (Page 46, 47)

Harry finds out that his mom and dad were famous wizards. Hagrid, Keeper of the Keys, at Hogwarts explains everything to Harry and finally hands Harry his letter of acceptance to Hogwarts School of Witchcraft and Wizardry. (Page 50, 51)

Hagrid tells of the killing of Harry's parents ten years ago on Halloween. (Page 54, 55)

Hagrid describes what happened to Voldemort after he tried to kill Harry. (Page 57)

Hagrid shows up again on the day after Harry's birthday and takes Harry to London to Diagon Alley, a magical place hidden from the Muggles where witches and wizards shop and where all Hogwarts students go to buy their school supplies. (Page 63,64,65)

Harry's list of items needed for 1st year students. (Page 66,67)

Harry enters Diagon Alley for the first time and is astonished by what he sees. (Page 71,72)

Harry buys his magic wand at Ollivander's Magic Wand Shop and finds out that his wand and Voldemort's wand are 'brothers'. Both wands were made from the same phoenix tail feather. The wand chooses the wizard. (Page 84, 85)

Harry leaves from Platform Nine and three-quarters at Kings Cross station on the last day of August. Harry overhears the Weasley family at the station and upon asking how to enter begins his journey to Hogwarts and meets the Weasley twins, Fred and George (Page 93, 94). Harry meets Ron Weasley for the first time (Page 98). Harry meets Hermione for the first time (Page 105,106). Harry meets Draco Malfoy for the first time. (Page 108).

Professor McGonagall, the deputy headmistress, announces the Sorting Hat Ceremony upon arrival at Hogwarts. Harry enters the Great Hall for the first time. (Page 116)

The Sorting Hat Ceremony begins with the Sorting Hat's song (Page 118) and Harry and his friends take part in the Sorting Hat Ceremony. (Page 119,120,121)

Hogwarts School Song (Page 128)

The professors are introduced. Professor Sprout - Biology; Professor Binns (a ghost) - History of Magic; Professor Flitwick - Charms; Professor McGonagall - Transfiguration; Professor Quirrell - Defense Against the Dark Arts; and Professor Snape - Potions. (Page 133,134)

Harry finds that Professor Snape, the Potions teacher, is a very critical teacher and it appears that he dislikes Harry. Snape's character is exposed somewhat. (Page 138,139)

The Remembrall glass ball from Neville's Gran is described. (Page 145)

Harry goes to his first flying broom lesson given by madam Hooch and finds out that he is a natural flyer. He has his first encounter with Draco Malfoy. (Page 146,147,148)

Harry and Draco agree to a Wizard's duel at Midnight in the Trophy room. Draco tells Professor Filch in an attempt to get Harry into trouble for being off-limits. As they flee from Filch they accidentally stumble into the forbidden corridor on the third floor where they encounter the three headed dog, Fluffy, who guards (they later find out) the entrance to the Sorcerer's Stone. (Page 160,161)

Quidditch is explained. Harry goes to the practice field to begin learning how to play Quidditch. The rules and play of the game are explained in detail. (Page 166,167,168,169)

On Halloween night it is announced that a troll is in the castle. Harry, Hermione and Ron follow Professor Snape who they see sneaking up to the third floor. Upon arriving, they encounter the troll. (Page 174,175,176)

Harry plays in his first Quidditch match. (Page 185 - 191)

Harry receives the invisibility cloak along with a very special note enclosed as a Christmas gift. (Page 201,202)

The Magnificent Mirror of Erised is found. Harry uses the invisibility cloak to enter the restricted section of the library. Professor Filch almost catches him but he hides in an unused classroom where he finds the Mirror of Erised. It is enscribed "I show not your face but your heart's desire" Harry looks at his parents for the first time in his life. (Page 207,208,209)

Professor Dumbledore describes the true meaning of the Mirror of Erised (Mirror of Desire). "It does not do to dwell on dreams and forget to live". (Page 213,214)

The identity of Nicolas Flamel is revealed in relationship to the Sorcerer's Stone. Nicolas Flamel is the only known maker of the Sorcerer's stone. (Page 219,220)

Gryffindor plays Hufflepuff in Quidditch (Page 222 - 224) After the game, Harry follows Snape into the forrest. Harry overhears Professor Quirrell and Professor Snape discussing how to get past the three-headed dog to find the Sorcerer's stone. (Page 226)

Harry, Hermione and Ron find out from Hagrid about Professor Dumbledore and the staff protecting the Sorcerer's Stone at Hogwarts. (Page 232)

Hagrid reveals that he is about to hatch a Norwegian Ridgeback Dragon egg. (Page 233) Harry, Malfoy, Hermione and Neville accompany Hagrid into the Forbidden Forrest where they encounter unicorn blood on the ground. (Page250)

The centaur Firenze saves Harry from the cloaked black figure (Voldemort) they found drinking the unicorn blood. (Page 256)

The mystery and essence of the unicorn blood is explained to Harry by Firenze, the centaur. Voldemort needs the unicorn blood in order to stay alive so he can find the Sorcerer's Stone that can provide the Elixir of Life. (Page 258,259)

Hagrid accidentally reveals the secret of how to get past Fluffy, the three headed dog, who is guarding the entrance to the hiding place of the Sorcerer's Stone. (Page 266)

Snape is the main suspect in the stealing of the Sorcerer's Stone. (Page 270)

Harry, Hermione and Ron approach Fluffy under the invisibility cloak in their quest to enter the chamber. (Page 275)

Hermione saves them from Devil's Snare, a flesh eating plant they encounter after dropping through the trapdoor. (Page 277, 278)

Harry uses his abilities he learned in Quidditch to capture a flying key. (280)

They must play a magical game of Chess in order to proceed to the chamber. (Page 281,282,283)

They must correctly solve a poem puzzle to proceed to the chamber. Hermione solves the puzzle. (Page 285,286)

Harry encounters the man with two faces and is surprised to find it is one of his professors. All of the mysteries are revealed to Harry. (Page 288,289,290)

The Mirror of Esired holds the key to the location of the Sorcerer's Stone. (Page 291,292)

Harry is confronted by Lord Voldemort and must now save himself from Voldemort. He must also keep Lord Voldemort from finding the stone. (Page 293,294)

Harry wakes up in the hospital wing. Professor Dumbledore explains what happened to Harry, Lord Voldemort and the Stone. (Page 296,297)

Dumbledore knows why Voldemort wants to kill Harry and reveals why and how he exists. We also learn who gave Harry the invisibility cloak for Christmas. (Page 298,299)

Dumbledore reveals the hiding place of the Sorcerer's Stone to Harry and the mystery of the Sorcerer's stone is solved. (Page 300)

Good always triumphs over evil in the end. Love has an enduring power over evil and by keeping faith in ourselves and practicing the powers of love, we can all defeat the dark forces that arise from time to time in all of our lives.

SORCERER'S STONE
CONCLUSION SCENE

The Chamber of Secrets, the second book in the series, follows *The Sorcerer's Stone* and continues Harry's adventures. After another hideous summer with his Muggle relatives, the Dursleys, Harry returns to Hogwarts. Before his return, Harry is visited by a strange, imp-like creature named Dobby who warns that if he returns to school, he will be struck with disaster.

Gilderoy Lockhart, an outlandishly vain professor, and Moaning Myrtle, a ghost who haunts the girls' bathroom, provide mystery and humor in Harry's second adventure. Ginny, Ron Weasley's little sister, attending Hogwarts for the first time and Harry's ardent admirer, becomes an important character in the mystery of *The Chamber of Secrets*.

Draco Malfoy, a student at Hogwarts and Harry's arch rival, becomes more and more of a problem as Hogwarts' students begin turning to stone and Harry becomes the prime suspect. Rubius Hagrid's mysterious past at Hogwarts is finally revealed and we find that once again Lord Voldemort is trying to regain his powers. The Chamber of Secrets is well hidden within the Hogwarts Castle, and once opened, it provides the reader with many clues to the past, present, and future.

At Hogwarts, Harry learns through reading a magical diary about Lord Voldemort's youth, how he was drawn to the Dark side, and that Lord Voldemort's Muggle name was Tom Marvolo Riddle. The reader also learns in *The Chamber of Secrets* that Harry and Voldemort have a lot in common: they are both Parsemouths (able to talk to snakes), both are half-bloods, both were raised by muggles, and both were orphaned at a young age. Also in this book, we learn more of Hogwart's history, and we also learn more about the four great wizards who started the school.

We find ourselves solidly immersed in the daily life at Hogwarts as we learn more and more of the past which in turn reveals yet more clues as the story unfolds. The author continues to develop the magical world by introducing new people, new places and magical creatures.

Dobby, a small house elf with bat-like ears, visits Harry at the Dursley's, the summer before his 2nd term. He warns Harry that he must not return to Hogwarts. (Page 16)

Ron Weasley appears at # 4 Privet Drive, rescues Harry from the Dursley's cellar, where he has been imprisoned, and takes him home to the Borough to spend the balance of the summer with the Weasley family before the new term begins. (Page 27)

The unusual garden gnomes in the Weasleys' Garden are introduced. (Page 37)

Using magical Floo Power, Harry travels to Diagon Alley with the Weasleys to purchase his school supplies. There he encounters Dracus Malfoy, and an important clue is revealed. Dracus instigates a fight with Arthur Weasley to cause a diversion and an opportunity to slip the magical diary in with their books. J. K. Rowling includes these and other subtle clues which challenge the reader's memory and intellect until the conclusion of each story. (Page 62,63)

Harry and Ron crash into the Whomping Willow at Hogwarts in the Weasley's Flying Ford, Anglia, arriving somewhat late, after missing the Hogwarts Express. (Page 74,75)

Gilderoy Lockhart is the new professor of Defense Against the Dark Arts at Hogwarts in Harry's 2nd year. He is characterized as somewhat of a vain fool. (Page 99,100)

The strange voice that only Harry can hear begins to haunt him. Harry's scar burns when he hears it. "It was a voice, a voice to chill the bone marrow, a voice of breath-taking, ice-cold venom". (Page 120)

The Deathday Party sets the stage for Harry to encounter the first of the assaults that begin on the Muggle born students at Hogwarts. Nearly Headless Nick, the ghost of Griffindor Tower, invites Harry and his friends to the Deathday Party on Halloween, deep in the dungeons of the castle, in celebration of his five hundredth Deathday. (Page 131 - 136)

Moaning Myrtle, the ghost, is introduced. (Page 132)

Harry again hears the same cold, murderous voice. (Page 137,138)

The Chamber of Secrets is opened and the caretaker's cat is found hanging by her tail from the torch bracket. (Page 139) Professor Dumbledore finds the caretaker, Mrs. Norris, petrified. (Page 142).

The Chamber of Secrets Legend is revealed. We learn that Salazar Slytherin was the creator. (Page 150,151)

Harry, Hermione and Ron decide to make a Polyjuice Potion to transform themselves into Draco Malfoys friends in order to learn if Draco is truly the heir to Slytherin. (Page 159)

The first Quidditch match of the year, Slytherin vs. Griffindor, begins with foul play. A rogue Bludger attacks Harry for no reason and almost kills him. (Page 167,168,169, 170, 171,172)

Harry goes to the Hogwarts hospital where Dobby, the elf, visits him for the second time and warns him of danger. The secret of the Rogue Bludger that attacked Harry is revealed and Dobby confirms the existence of the Chamber of Secrets. (Page 176,177,178)

Colin Creevey is attacked and petrified holding a camera in his hands. This is the second attack on a Muggle since the Chamber of Secrets was opened. (Page 180)

A dueling club is started by Professor Lockhart. Harry and Draco face off for the first time with wands and magic. (Page 192, 193) Harry is attacked by Draco a second time and when a snake attacks Harry, he learns that he is a Parsemouth. (Page 195)

Harry visits Professor Dumbledore's secret office and learns why the Sorting Hat placed him in Gryffindor instead of Slytheryn. Harry also meets Fawkes, Professor Dumbledore's Phoenix and learns the secrets of the Phoenix. Many clues are given during this visit which will be used in the conclusion. (Page 205,206,207)

Justin Finch-Fletchley is found rigid and cold on the floor next to the remains of Nearly Headless Nick, the ghost of Gryffindor. No mortal or ghost is safe from attack. (Page 202) What terrible power was invoked that could harm someone who was already dead?

Harry, Hermione and Ron finally brew the Polyjuice Potion during Christmas and change themselves into Malfoy's friends in the girls bathroom with Moaning Myrtle present. They proceed to find Malfoy intending to learn if he is the person responsible for the attacks. (Page 216,217)

Harry finds the secret diary in the girls bathroom. (Page 229,230)

The blank diary of T. M. Riddle, an early student at Hogwarts is revealed. (Page 232,233)

Harry discovers the secret to Riddle's Diary. (Page 240,241)

The secret diary begins to talk to Harry and tells the story of Tom Riddle, the original owner. (Page 242,243, 244, 245, 246, 247)

The secret voice in Harry's head manifests itself again. (Page 254)

There is an attack on two students, Hermione and a Ravenclaw student. Hermione is found holding a circular mirror. Another important clue is presented that will later be explained why Hermione is petrified and not killed. (Page 257)

With the aid of the invisibility cloak that Harry inherited from his father, Harry and Ron visit Hagrid in his cottage in the forest late at night. Remaining invisible in the cottage they witness a visit by Dumbledore, Cornelius Fudge, and later by Dracus Malfoy. Hagrid is removed to Azkaban the wizard prison and Professor Dumbledore is relieved from his position as Head Master by Dracus Malfoy. (Page 260,261, 262)

Dumbledore provides an important clue upon leaving Hagrid Cottage while Harry and Ron are still hidden by the invisibility cloak. (Page 263,264) Dumbledore's message is repeated on page 266.

Harry and Ron venture into the Forbidden Forest protected by the invisibility cloak. They are following the trail of the spiders, which Harry concluded from earlier clues, would lead them to the secret entrance of the chamber. In the forest they meet Aragog and learn about Hagrid's expulsion from Hogwarts despite his innocence. They also learn of the mystery of the monster in the chamber. (Page 276,277,278)

The monster that dwells in the Chamber of Secrets is described in an old library page that Harry discovers in the hand of the petrified Hermione in the hospital wing. (Page 290).

Harry, after putting all the pieces together, tells Ron why all the attacks so far have only petrified the victims instead of killing them. (Page 292)

Harry discovers the entrance to the Chamber of Secrets. (Page 292)

The Heir of Slytherin leaves a message that Ginny Weasley has been taken by the monster. "Her skeleton will lie in the Chamber forever". (Page 293)

The secret of Moaning Myrtle is revealed. (Page 299)

Harry, Ron, and Professor Lockhart find the entrance to the Chamber of Secrets and enter. (Page 300,301)

Tom Riddle appears in the Chamber of Secrets and reveals the secrets of the diary (which Harry has lost) and explains how the diary helped to bring him back to life. (Page 307,308,309)

The person who opened the Chamber of Secrets is revealed. (Page 310)

The expulsion and framing of Hagrid is explained. (Page 311,312)

The truth about Lord Voldemort and Tom Riddle is revealed. (Page 314)

Dumbledore sends the Sorting Hat and Fawkes (his Phoenix bird) to Harry as defensive weapons against the monster. (Page 315)

Tom Riddle summons the monster and a clue as to his identity is revealed. (Page 317)

The Sorting Hat saves Harry from the monster. (Page 319,320)

Fawkes, the Phoenix, saves Harry's life. (Page 321,322)

Harry discloses the entire story to Professor Dumbledore and solves the unanswered questions and gaps in the adventure in Dumbledore's office. (Page 327,328,329)

The Good vs. Evil theme of the Harry Potter books is described by Professor Dumbledore to Harry. (Page 333)

Lucius Malfoy, young Draco's father, appears in Dumbledore's office with Dobby, his house elf. Harry confronts Malfoy with the truth about the diary and his involvement with everything that has occurred. Dobby helps to reveal the truth. (Page 335,336)

Harry, through clever thoughtfulness, releases Dobby from the Malfoy household. (Page 337,338)

The clever writing and hidden messages and clues of J. K. Rowling are again highlighted when Harry asks Dobby a final question. (Page 339)

The truth about the blood left on the sheet of Ron's bed when Scabbers was missing is revealed. (Page 364)

The truth about the Secret Keeper is revealed. (Page 365)

Scabbers is forced by magic spells to transform back into Peter Pettigrew which will reveal his true identity. (Page 366)

Sirius Black reveals how he escaped from Azkaban. (Page 371)

Peter Pettigrew confesses that he is Voldemort's follower and was responsible for killing James and Lilly Potter. (Page 374)

Harry prevents Lupin and Black from killing Pettigrew. (Page 375)

Harry Potter learns about the principles of Good vs. Evil.   If he allows Pettigrew to be killed, he becomes no better than Voldemort. Saving Pettigrew's life, demonstrates he has risen above the need to avenge his parent's death.   (Page 376)

Harry speaks with Dumbledore regarding the truth about Sirius Black. Dumbledore provides an important clue that will save Sirius Black from the pending Dementor's kiss. Time is the key (Page 392,393)

Hermione figures out Dumbledore's clue and reveals the "time-turner". By going back in time they can save more than one life; Buckbeak is saved from the executioner.. (Page 394-402)

Harry solves the mystery of why the "Expecto Patronum" spell worked to save himself from the dementors who were about to preform the 'dementor kiss' on Harry by the lake. (Page 410,411)

Sirius Black is saved by Harry and Hermione with the help of Buckbeak and the spell of the "time-turner". (Page 413,414,415)

Professor Snap accuses Harry of helping Black to escape. (Page 419, 420)

Professor Lupin leaves Hogwarts and gives Harry back the Invisibility Cloak and the Marauder's Map. Professor Dumbledore arrives and bids Lupin farewell. (Page 424,425)

Dumbledore tells Harry that by saving Pettigrew's life, it creates a bond that may return in the future. (Page 426,427)

Harry receives an Owl Post from Sirius Black. (Page 432,433)

Harry puts Uncle Vernon on notice that Sirius Black is his Godfather. (Page 434,435)

THE FAT LADY
(ENTRANCE TO GRYFFINDOR TOWER)

CHAMBER OF SECRETS
CONCLUSION SCENE

✳ ✳

✳ ✳

* 31 *

SYNOPSIS

The Prisoner of Azkaban is the third book in the Harry Potter series and tells of Harry's 3rd year at Hogwarts. In this book, we learn about the terrible prison fortress of Azkaban where the dark and sinister followers of Lord Voldemort are held. It is the worst place to be sent. The guards there are the Dementors whose special talent is to suck the soul out of a body, leaving no memory, no sense of self, no . . . anything. What can an escaped prisoner be like and what is he capable of?

The Prisoner of Azkaban introduces Sirius Black, a main supporting character. Sirius Black, reported heir apparent to Lord Voldemort, and convicted of killing thirteen people with a single curse, has escaped after twelve long years in Azkaban. The best clue to his whereabouts is that the guards at Azkaban heard Black muttering in his sleep, "He's at Hogwarts . . . He's at Hogwarts."

In this book we learn a wealth of history and information that binds together the first two novels' characters, places and things. The new information provides us with a history of events that have led up to the present time.

This book also introduces the Marauder's Map, a complete map of Hogwarts which reveals the current location of every resident.

Sirius Black is coming to Hogwarts and Harry Potter must heed the warnings he has received from numerous sources. Who is Sirius Black? Hagrid was riding Black's motorcycle when she brought the baby Harry to Dumbledore for protection from Voldemort! How was Black related to Hagrid or to the Potter family? What did Black do to become a prisoner in the horrible Azkaban prison? He has now escaped and is reportedly coming to Hogwarts . . . it is rumored that he is or was a death eater and is coming to kill Harry!

Unlike the first two novels where Lord Voldemort is introduced and developed as the villain, the Prisoner of Azkaban provides a stable platform of information, revealing past history and unifying the first two novels. A new villain has arrived . . . Sirius Black!

During Harry's 3rd summer, he receives a message by Owl Post that the Weasley family has won a drawing and they have decided to vacation in Egypt. (Page 8)

Aunt Marge visits the Dursleys and Harry promises to act like a Muggle in return for Uncle Vernon signing a permission slip from Hogwarts to enable Harry to visit Hogsmeade during the school year. But Aunt Marge angers Harry by insulting his dead parents and Harry retaliates with a magical charm causing Uncle Vernon to recant. (Page 29)

Harry leaves #4 Privet Drive at night in a rage. The Knight Bus, a magical emergency transport for stranded witches or wizards, appears and takes Harry away. (Page 33,34,35)

Harry learns about Sirius Black's escape from Azkaban Prison from The Daily Profit newspaper on the Knight Bus. (Page 37,38)

Harry asks Ernie, the bus driver, to take him to the Leaky Cauldron (Diagon Alley entrance) and upon arrival is surprised to find the Minister of Magic, Cornelius Fudge, waiting for him. (Page 42)

Fudges places Harry in a room at the Leaky Cauldron for the two weeks before school starts and advises Harry to confine himself to Diagon Alley for safety. Harry finds the fastest broom in the Quality Quidditch Supplies shop, a FIREBOLT, capable of 150 miles an hour acceleration! (Page 50,51)

Harry meets up with Hermione and the Weasleys and they all attend a dinner together at the Leaky Cauldron. Rumors that Sirius Black is after Harry surface. (Page 66,67)

Harry encounters a Dementor on the Hogwarts Express as they all set off for their third year at Hogwarts. Professor Lupin uses a spell to make the Dementor from Azakaban leave their train car. (Page 83,84,85)

Harry arrives at Hogwarts and at the welcome dinner, Rubius Hagrid is promoted to Care of Magical Creatures teacher. (Page 93)

Draco Malfoy, Harry's arch enemy in the student body, continues to taunt and make fun of Harry. (Page 99)

Harry, Ron and Hermione meet the bumbling Knight Sir Cadogan, who leads them to Sibyll Trelawney, the Divination teacher. Professor Trelawney is always penetrating the future to unveil mysteries. (Page 100)

Professor Trelawney informs Harry he has the Grim, an omen of death. (Page 107)

Hagrid teaches his first Care of Magical Creatures Class and shows students how to open The Book of Monsters. Harry and Draco continue to taunt each other in class. Meanwhile, Hagrid introduces Buckbeak, a hippogriff (half horse and half bird). (Page 113,114,115)

Malfoy insults Buckbeak, something Hagrid had warned against; Draco Malfoy is injured and the Slytherins accuse Hagrid of being incompetent because of the incident. (Page 118)

Seamus Finnigan, Crabbe, Goyle, and Draco Malfoy continue to taunt Harry while they make potions and formulas in Professor Snape's class on Potions. Sirius Black is reported to be near by. (Page 124, 125,126, 127)

Hermione, while leaving Snape's class with Harry and Ron, disappears and then reappears. (Page 129)

Professor Lupin, the Defense Against the Dark Arts teacher, provides some humor and places a "Waddiwasi" spell on Peeves the Poltergeist, who constantly causes havoc around the castle. (Page 131)

Professor Lupin instructs the class on Boggarts, shape-shifters that assume the shape of the victim's greatest fear. He teaches the class the "riddikulus" charm that repels a Boggart. (Page 133, 134, 135)

Because Harry doesn't have a parental pass to go to Hogsmeade for Halloween with the other students, Professor Lupin invites Harry into his office. Lupin shows Harry the grindylows which are water demon creatures. During this visit to Lupin's office, subtle information is revealed which will have an impact on the conclusion. (Page 153,154, 155,156,157)

The Fat Lady is attacked in her portrait and runs away to hide in a map of Argyllshire on the second floor. Peeves the Poltergeist reports that it was Sirius Black. (Page 160,161)

Sir Cadogan, the knight, replaces the Fat Lady as the Gryffindor guardian, and because he is a lunatic, he is always challenging people to duels and thinking up complicated passwords. (Page 167)

Harry and the Gryffindors play Hufflepuff for a house Quidditch match in a rain storm. Harry crashes in the ground after being attacked by a hundred Dementors focusing on him thus causing him to hear screams in his head during the match. (Page 176, 177, 178, 179, 180)

Harry receives the Marauder's Map from Fred and George, the Weasley twins. (Page 191, 192) The secret to the Marauder's Map is disclosed and many of the secret passages to Hogsmeade are revealed. (Page 193)

Harry uses the invisibility cloak and the Maurader's map to go to Hogsmeade. (Page 195,196)

Harry learns while invisible at Hogsmeade that his father, James Potter was Sirius Black's best friend. But Sirius Black is reported to be in league with Voldemort. Sirius Black had been the Secret-Keeper of the Fidelius Charm that protected the Potters. Black is Harry's Godfather and it appears that his parents had been betrayed by their best friend. (Page 203,204,205,206)

Peter Pettigrew, who hero-worshipped Serius Black and James Potter, is introduced and we learn of his demise. (Page 207,208)

Cornelius Fudge describes the scene after the murder of numerous wizards. Sirius Black is the accused assassin. (Page 208)

Harry plans vengeance against Sirius Black for what Black reportedly did to his family. (Page 214,215)

Hagrid is notified that he must report to the school governors about the Hippogriff attack on Malfoy and becomes despondent. (Page 217, 218, 219)

Harry receives a new FIREBOLT broomstick from a mysterious source. (Page 223)

Professor Lupin is suddenly reported ill and continues to be failing. (Page 229)

Harry's new FIREBOLT is confiscated by Professor McGonagall and inspected for jinxes. It is suspected that it was sent by Sirius Black. (Page 233)

Professor Lupin uses a Boggart to teach the Patronus Charm to Harry and the class. The Patronus Charm is a very advanced charm that will have an important bearing in the conclusion. (Page 236 - 242)

Professor Lupin explains the Dementor's Kiss. (Page 247)

Ron Weasley suspects Hermione's cat Crookshanks is responsible for Scabbers (Ron's pet rat) disappearing and leaving only a blood spot. (Page 251)

Colin Creevey, a second year student who is deeply in awe of Harry, is introduced. He is always taking pictures of Harry. (Page 152)

The Quidditch match between Gryffindor and Ravenclaw begins with Harry riding the new FIREBOLT. The Dementors show up again and Harry uses the Patronus Charm to prevent a repeat accident. (Page 259 - 263)

Ron Weasley declares that Sirius Black appeared in the dormitory and slashed the curtains with a knife. (Page 266,267,268)

Professors Snape's grudge is revealed.   Snape finds the Marauder's Map in Harry's pocket and attempts to find out its secret. Professor Lupin appears to end the questioning   and confiscates the map.   (Page 284,285,286,287,288)

Harry sees Crookshanks, Hermione's cat, and a big black shaggy dog moving across the lawn outside his window. (Page 303,304)

Slytherin vs. Gryffindor - The exciting Quidditch Match Final.   (Page 306 - 313)

Professor Trelawney' Prediction - The Dark Lord is going to rise again. (Page 322,323,324)

Scabbers the pet rat is acting funny, and Crookshanks is chasing him. The big shaggy dog appears and drags Ron away and disappears into a secret passage within the Whomping Willow. (Page 334,335)

Crookshanks presses a knot on the Whomping Willow that freezes the tree and opens a portal to the Shrieking Shack. Harry and Hermione follow. (Page 336)

Sirius Black confronts Harry, Hermione and Ron in the Shrieking Shack. Harry has the opportunity to kill Black. (Page 338 - 342)

Professor Lupin appears in the Shrieking Shack and disarms everyone's wand. Professor Lupin reveals his true identity. (Page 343,344,345)

Professor Lupin explains the Marauder's Map and what it has revealed. (Page 347,348)

The truth about Peter Pettigrew is revealed. (Page 348)

The truth about the Whomping Willow and the Shrieking Shack is revealed. (Page 353)

We learn the truth about Padfoot, Wormtail, and Prongs, the nicknames on the Marauder's Map. (Page 354,355)

Professor Snape appears and we learn about the trick that Sirius Black played upon him long ago at Hogwarts. (Page 356,357)

Professor Snape takes charge and renders Professor Lupin motionless. Snape is convinced that Lupin and Black are there to kill Harry. (Page 359)

Harry exposes Snape for the first time. Snape is seeking vengeance because he was made a fool of while he was in school with Black and Lupin. (Page 361)

The truth about Ron's pet rat Scabbers is revealed. (Page 363)

The truth about the blood left on the sheet of Ron's bed when Scabbers was missing is revealed. (Page 364)

The truth about the Secret Keeper is revealed. (Page 365)

Scabbers is forced by magic spells to transform back into Peter Pettigrew which will reveal his true identity. (Page 366)

Sirius Black reveals how he escaped from Azkaban. (Page 371)

Peter Pettigrew confesses that he is Voldemort's follower and was responsible for killing James and Lilly Potter. (Page 374)

Harry prevents Lupin and Black from killing Pettigrew. (Page 375)

Harry Potter learns about the principles of Good vs. Evil. If he allows Pettigrew to be killed, he becomes no better than Voldemort. Saving Pettigrew's life, demonstrates he has risen above the need to avenge his parent's death. (Page 376)

Harry speaks with Dumbledore regarding the truth about Sirius Black. Dumbledore provides an important clue that will can save Sirius Black from the pending Dementor's kiss. Time is the key. (Page 392,393)

Hermione figures out Dumbledore's clue and reveals the "time-turner". By going back in time they can save more than one life; Buckbeak is saved from the executioner. (Page 394-402)

Harry solves the mystery of why the "Expecto Patronum" spell worked to save himself from the dementors who were about to perform the 'dementor kiss' on Harry by the lake. (Page 410,411)

Sirius Black is saved by Harry and Hermione with the help of Buckbeak and the spell of the "time-turner". (Page 413,414,415)

Professor Snape accuses Harry of helping Black to escape. (Page 419, 420)

Professor Lupin leaves Hogwarts and gives Harry back the Invisibility Cloak and the Marauder's Map. Professor Dumbledore arrives and bids Lupin farewell. (Page 424,425)

Dumbledore tells Harry that by saving Pettigrew's life, it creates a bond that may return in the future. (Page 426,427)

Harry receives an Owl Post from Sirius Black. (Page 432,433)

Harry puts Uncle Vernon on notice that Sirius Black is his Godfather. (Page 434,435)

THE GOLDEN SNITCH

PRISONER OF AZKABAN
CONCLUSION SCENE

The Goblet of Fire is the fourth book in the Harry Potter series. It begins with the Riddle House chapter where we see Lord Voldemort return to his boyhood home, using the empty old house for a sanctuary. Wormtail, his loyal follower, sustains Voldemort by milking Nagani, the Great Balsik snake accompanying them, to nourish Voldemort's lifeless-vapor form. It is in this pivotal fourth novel that we see how Voldemort's ruthlessness is evident, both in the past and in the present. We learn of his plans to return to power and kill Harry. We are alerted from the beginning that Voldemort is coming and has made extensive plans to use the Tri-Wizard Tournament as his means of trapping Harry. The stage is set for Voldemort and Harry to face one another for the first time since Voldemort tried to kill him as an infant. Harry, still a fledgling wizard-to-be, will have to fight for his very life.

Harry Potter is now 14 years old and preparing to return to a very special year at Hogwarts. He is invited to attend the International Quidditch World Cup Tournament with Ron, Hermione and the Weasleys. This exciting event is a wonderful time for Harry and gives the reader an insight into the magical world of witches and wizards. We also learn about numerous magical items, some of which will become crucial later in the tale, including The Dark Mark, Voldemort's sign, which appears for the first time after the match.

When Harry arrives at the Hogwarts school, there is excitement in the air. Something special is going to happen at Hogwarts in this his fourth year. The school's intramural Quidditch Cup Matches have been suspended and, for the first time in 100 years, Hogwarts is to host the Tri-Wizard Tournament! This is an annual tournament between three of the most renowned wizard schools, Hogwarts, Beaxbatons and Durmstrang. Each school chooses one student to compete in a series of three serious and oft-times dangerous events. Little does Harry know that not only will he become one of the contestants but also that his life will be in danger, for Lord Voldemort has been plotting to kill Harry Potter using the tournament to his advantage.

The gardener to the Riddle house, Frank, is introduced and is blamed for the mysterious deaths of the Riddles. (Page 2,3,4)

Frank, now the caretaker, investigates a strange light in the old house and eaves-drops upon Voldemort and Wormtail. (Page 6,7)

Voldemort, with Wormtail's help, plots his return. We learn of the Quidditch World Tournament and Voldemort's determination to kill Harry. (Page 7,8,9)

Voldemort's plan is partially revealed. (Page 10,11)

Voldemort discovers Frank, the gardener, and invites him into the room. We learn more about Voldemort and his ruthless capabilities. (Page 14,15)

The lightening bolt scar on Harry's forehead begins to hurt. This scar is a link to Voldemort and allows Harry a brief glimpse of what Voldemort is doing. (Page 17)

Harry writes to his godfather, Sirius Black the ex-prisoner of Azkaban, and tells him about his scar hurting and the possible existence of Voldemort nearby. (Page 25)

The invitation letter for Harry to attend the Quidditch World Cup with the Weasley's, arrives at the Dursleys. (Page 30)

Using magical Foo Powder, the Weasleys arrive in the Dursley's fireplace at #4 Privet Drive, but find the fireplace blocked. (Page 42,43,44)

Ton-Tongue Toffee is left behind by the Weasley twins as a joke, and Dudley finds out it is more than just toffee. (Page 49)

Weasley's Wizard Wheezes are revealed as Joke stuff that the Weasley twins have been inventing in their spare time. (Page 54,55)

Harry learns that they will travel to the International Quidditch Match via a magical "Portkey". They leave from Stoatshead Hill. (Page 70,71,72,73)

Victor Krum, the Bulgarian Seeker, is introduced. (Page 83)

Ludo Bagman, from the department of Magical Games and responsible for the Quidditch tickets, is introduced to everyone. He is the game announcer and the Head of the Department of Magical Games and Sports. (Page 86,87,88,89)

Barty Couch is introduced and arrives to join Bagman and the Weasleys. Couch, in addition to his normal duties as Head of the Department of International Magical Cooperation at the Ministry of Magic, is responsible for organizing the Portkeys. (Page 90,91,92)

The first hint of the Tri-Wizard Tournament at Hogwarts is discussed. (Page 92)

Winky, Barty Crouch's house elf, is introduced. Winky is also a friend of Dobby, ex-house elf of the Malfoys. (Page 97,98,99)

The International Quidditch Match begins with Ireland vs. Bulgaria, with Victor Krum, the international seeker star, playing for Bulgaria. (Page 105 - 113)

The Dark Mark appears in the forest after the Quidditch Match. Harry, Ron and Hermione leave the campsite and venture into the nearby woods for protection as the excitement and celebration of the Match has turned into chaos. (Page 128,129)

The mystery of the Dark Mark is discussed. How did it appear and who summoned it? (Page 130 - 138)

Mayhem at the Ministry of Magic is highlighted. Rita Skeeter, the nosy reporter, is investigating the disappearance of Bertha Jorkin, an employee missing for several months. (Page 153)

Harry learns about Mad-eye Moody during a discussion in the Weasley home just prior to leaving for his fourth term at Hogwarts. (Page 161)

Professor Dumbledore begins the fall term. Mad-Eye Moody, the new Defense Against the Dark Arts teacher, arrives. (Page 184,185)

Professor Dumbledore announces the Triwizard Tournament and the tournament is discussed. (Page 186,187)

Rules of Entering the Triwizard Tournament are revealed. (Page 188)

Bubotubers, thick, black, giant slugs-like plants are introduced in Professor Sprouts class. (Page 194,195)

Blast-Ended Skrewts are described in Hagrid's class for Magical Creatures. (Page 196,197)

Rita Skeeter continues to use The Daily Prophet newspaper to embarrass Arthur Weasley in his position in the Ministry of Magic. (Page 202,203)

Malfoy attacks Harry while his back is turned. Mad-Eye Moody appears and deals with Malfoy by turning him into a ferret as punishment. (Page 204,205,206)

The Unforgivable Curses are described by Professor Moody in the Defense Against the Dark Arts Class. (Page 211)

The Impero Curse is shown to Ron Weasley by Professor Moody. (Page 212,213)

The Cruciatus Curse is shown to Neville Longbottom by Professor Moody. (Page 214,215)

The Avada Kedavra Curse is shown to Hermione Granger by Professor Moody. (Page 215,216)

The Unforgivable curses are identified and Moody warns against them. (Page 217)

S.P.E.W. - Society for the Promotion of Elfish Welfare. Hermione decides on a campaign to free the house elves. (Page 224,225)

Beauxbaton School arrives at Hogwarts. Professor Madame Maxime is the headmaster. (Page242,243,244)

Durmstrang School arrives at Hogwarts with Professor Igor Kararoff, headmaster. (Page 246,247)

Professor Dumbledore explains the Triwizard Tournament. (Page 253,254,255)

The Goblet of Fire appears in the Great Hall. (Page 255, 256)

Mad-Eye Moody and Kararoff meet for the first time in many years. (Page 258)

The champions are chosen by the Goblet of Fire after the Great Halloween Feast. Viktor Krum for Durmstrang; Fleur Delacour for Beauxbaton; Cedric Diggory for Hufflepuff/Hogwarts; and Harry Potter for Gryffindor/Hogwarts. (Page 267 - 271)

Mad-Eye Moody theorizes why Harry Potter's name appeared from the Goblet of Fire. (Page 278,279,280)

Information regarding the first task of the Triwizard Tournament is revealed. (Page 280,281)

Rita Skeeter drags Harry into a small closet and proceeds to interview him. (Page 303,304,305,306)

Professor Dumbledore rescues Harry from Rita Skeeter's interview in the closet. The Weighing of the Wands ceremony begins. (Page 307)

Mr. Ollivander, owner of Ollivander's Wand Shop in Diagon Alley, examines each of the champion's wands. (Page 308,309,310,311)

Hagrid leads Madame Maxim and Harry (Harry is disguised under the Invisibility Cloak) into The Forbidden Forest to see the four dragons to be used in the first task. The Hungarian Horntail Dragon is introduced. (Page 325,326,327,328)

Harry meets with Sirius Black in the fireplace in Gryffindor house. Sirius reveals to Harry that Karkaroff was a Death Eater and was released from Azkaban. Sirius discusses Rita Skeeter, Bertha Jorkins, Mad-Eye Moody, Karkaroff and the events confronting Harry including the first task. (Page 331,332,333,334)

Mad-Eye Moody helps Harry with clues to the first task. Hermione helps Harry to prepare. (Page 344,345)

Ludo Bagman reveals the first task. (Page 349,350)

Harry demonstrates his character and fair play by declining Ludo Bagman's help (outside help is against the rules) at the last minute. (Page 351)

The First Triwizard Task. (Page351-356)

Ron, Hemimone and Harry visit the Hogwart kitchens where the house elves work. Harry meets Winky and Dobby again. Dobby and Winky provide additional clues to the unsolved mysteries. (Page375-382)

Harry finds out about the unexpected task of dancing, the opening dance of the Yule Ball at The Christmas Feast. (Page 401,402)

Professor Dumbledore provides an insight into the mysteries of Hogwarts. He reinforces that Hogwarts is an ever changing castle; the rooms randomly continue to appear and change locations. (Page 417)

Harry and Parvati open the dance at the Yule Ball with the other champions. (Page 419,420)

Cedric Diggory gives Harry a clue to the mystery of the Dragon Egg. A clue given to each of the champions for the second Triwizard Task.. (Page 431)

Rita Skeeter's article appears in the Daily Prophet. It damages both Dumbledore and Hagrid with her erroneous reporting. (Page 437,438,439,440)

Ludo Bagman meets with Harry and discloses that Barty Crouch is missing from the Ministry. Additional clues are offered by Bagman to help Harry (Bagman encourages cheating) in the tournament. (Page 445,446,447)

Hagrid reveals that his parents were Giants. He is depressed about the Rita Skeeter newspaper article. (Page 455,456)

Harry visits Moaning Myrtle in the Girls Bathroom and learns the secret to the golden egg. The clue to the second task is revealed. (Page 459-463)

Harry learns that there are "Merpeople" creatures that dwell in the lake, from Moaning Myrtle. (Page 464)

The Marauder's Map reveals peculiar behavior involving Barty Crouch in Snape's office. (Crouch is too ill to attend other functions but found prowling around in the Castle. Harry investigates. (Page 466, 467)

Harry being invisible, encounters Filch, the caretaker, and drops the golden egg (the champions' clue to the next task) while looking at the Mauraders map. Snape shows up and Mad-Eye Moody appears shortly thereafter. Moody bails Harry out of the situation, retrieves the egg from Snape and Filch and discusses the mysteries with Harry. Moody provides a important clue to Harry's possible future. (Page 477)

Dobby reveals a secret to Harry regarding the second task about the Merpeople and a special substance called "gillyweed". (Page 490,491)

The Second Triwizard Task is revealed and Ludo Bagman starts the second task. (Page493 - 503)

The Merchieftainess Murcus, chief of the Merpeople, discloses the events as they occurred while the champions were underwater to Bagman. The points are awarded. (Page 506,507)

Harry demonstrates not only courage but moral fiber. (Page 507)

Harry, Ron and Hermione go to Hogsmeade to meet Sirius Black, disguised as a shaggy dog, known in past novels as "Padfoot". (Page 520,521)

The condition of Barty Crouch is discussed. Crouch's condition plays an important role that is identified in the end chapter. (Page 522,523)

Sirius Black discusses all of the current mysteries with Harry, Ron and Hermione. This is an important recap of what has happened in addition to questions that in effect, are clues to many of the mysteries and events to come. (Page 524 - 533)

Winky, Crouch's house elf, reveals more information regarding the mysteries surrounding Barty Crouch. (Page 536,537,538)

Rita Skeeter continues to write absurd tales about Harry-Krum-Hermione and of course all of the past tales in the Daily Prophet. Hermione receives "hate mail" and begins to investigate how Rita Skeeter is getting the information. (Page 546,547)

Crouch continues to be "missing in action". (Page 549) Crouch is discovered wandering and possibly out of his mind on the Hogwarts grounds. (Page 553 - 557)

Crouch attacks Viktor Krum, the Durmstrang champion and disappears. Mysteries continue surrounding Barty Crouch. (Page 560,561)

Dumbledore demonstrates his knowledge of what is happening and knows more than he ever reveals when he speaks to Harry. Professor Dumbledore is always there in the end to help Harry but only as a bystander. Always allowing Harry to face the mysteries and solve them for himself. Harry's guardian and behind the scenes mentor and teacher has always been Professor Dumbledore. (Page 562)

Further Clues to Barty Crouch are revealed. (Page 565)

Mad-Eye Moody provides a possible long range clue regarding Hermione Granger's vocation upon graduation from Hogwarts. (Page 570)

A letter from Sirius Black warns Harry that death is near. (Page 572)

Harry dreams in Professor Trelawney's Class. In his dream, Harry is in contact with Lord Voldemort. This is either a premonition or a link to what Voldemort and Wormtail are plotting. (Page 576, 577)

Harry discovers the Pensieve in Professor Dumbledore's office. When he looks into the shallow stone basin with odd carvings around the edges, a silvery light emanates from its contents. Harry disappears into the Pensieve just as Alice disappeared down the rabbit hole. Important answers, clues and mysteries are revealed as Harry witnesses important past events while in the Pensieve. (Page 583 - 596)

The mystery of the use of the Pensieve in Dumbledore's office is revealed. (It siphons the excess thoughts from one's mind and stores them for recall). (Page 597)

Dumbledore's philosophy, "Curiosity is not a sin, but we should exercise caution with our curiosity." (Page 598)

The mystery about Harry's scar hurting is revealed by Dumbledore. (Page 600)

The coming of Voldemort and his ascent to power is analyzed. It is marked with disappearances. (Page 601)

The background of Neville Longbottom is revealed. (Page 602, 603)

The mystery of Dumbledore's trust of Snape (once a supporter of the Dark Lord) is discussed. Dumbledore reaffirms that he trusts Snape, but the reasons are still not thoroughly revealed. (Page 604)

Rita Skeeter's article "Harry Potter - Disturbed and Dangerous" is featured in the Daily Prophet. Because of this article, Hermione is to solve the puzzle of how Rita Skeeter obtains the information she distorts. (Page 611, 612, 613, 614)

Another clue is revealed regarding Barty Crouch. Crouch is a key figure in the final chapter. (Page 618)

The third task of the Triwizard Tournament. (Page 620 - 628)

The Riddle of the sphinx must be solved in the third task. (Page 629, 630)

Harry and Cedric both reach the Triwizard Cup at the end of the Maze and are surprised at the outcome. (Page 631-635)

Cedric Diggory is transported with Harry to the old graveyard by the Portkey. Cedric is confronted by Voldemort. (Page 638)

Flesh, Blood, and Bone - Wormtail performs the ceremony to revive Lord Voldemort and Harry is bound helpless to the Riddle Tombstone. (Page 638 - 642)

Lord Voldemort Returns. (Page 643)

Voldemort recalls his parents and conjures up the Death Eaters (his followers). One by one they appear and form a circle surrounding Voldemort and Harry. (Page 646, 647)

Voldemort reveals his wrath. (Page 649)

Lucius Malfoy is revealed as a Death Eater. (Page 650)

Voldemort reveals that three Death Eaters are "dead in my service" and also reveals how he has managed to return at the request of Lucius Malfoy. (Page 651 - 657)

Voldemort reveals what happened to Bertha Jorkins. (Page 655)

Voldemort, being beaten once before by Harry as a baby through "ancient magic" used by Harry's mother, now declares he is the strongest. He frees Harry and returns Harry's wand to him for a duel to the death. (Page 658)

Voldemort and Harry Duel to the Death. (Page 660 - 669)

Moody learns of Harry's battle with Voldemort. (Page 673,674)

Moody reveals his secret to Harry. (Page 675,676,677,678)

Professor Dumbledore, Professor McGonagall and Professor Snape confront Mad-Eye Moody. Dumbledore's power as one of the greatest wizards is revealed and confirmed. (Page 679 - 681)

The real identity of Mad-Eye Moody is revealed. (Page 682,683)

The truth about Barty Crouch and his son are revealed. (Page 684,685)

The person who stole Harry's wand at the Quidditch World Cup is revealed. (Page 686)

Crouch's son reveals the secrets surrounding the Quidditch World Cup, Barty Crouchs' disappearance and Mad-Eye (Alastor) Moody. (Page 688, 689,690)

The secret of the Triwizard Cup is revealed. (Page 691)

Professor Dumbledore outlines the measures and steps that must be taken now that Voldemort has returned. (Page 707,708,709)

Snape reveals he was once a Death Eater. (Page 710)

Dumbledore outlines the steps now necessary to deal with the return of the Dark Lord. He gives directions that as yet are not fully revealed to the reader. (Page 712, 713)

Abbott, Hannah - "pink-faced girl with blonde pigtails"; Hufflepuff house

Agrippa - a wizard depicted on the Chocolate Frogs trading card; historically, a noted founder in the study of Alchemy

Archie - a very old wizard trying to pass as a Muggle wearing a long flowery nightgown

Aunt Marge - Uncle Vernon's sister; she hates Harry and openly insults Harry

Avery - a revealed Death Eater (GOF)

Basil - a wizard wearing a Muggle "kilt" at the World Cup

Bell, Katie - plays Chaser on the Gryffindor Quidditch team

Billius (also Uncle Billius) - Ron's uncle who saw a grim and died within 24 hours

Bode - a member of the Department of Mysteries

Bones, Susan - a student sorted into Hufflepuff

Boot, Terry - a student sorted into Ravenclaw

Brocklehurst, Mandy - a student sorted into Ravenclaw

Brown, Lavender - a student sorted into Gryffindor

Bryce, Frank - a gardener for the Riddle family, killed by Voldemort

Bulstrode, Millicent - Slytherin who duels Hermione in the Dueling Club demonstrations

GINNY WEASLEY

Chang, Cho - a Ravenclaw, plays Seeker on the Ravenclaw Quidditch team

Clearwater, Penelope - a Ravenclaw prefect and Percy Weasley's girlfriend

Crabbe, Vincent - Draco Malfoy's friend

Creevey, Colin - a year younger than Harry. Colin is in Gryffindor and Harry's biggest
admirer (after Ginny Weasley). Colin follows Harry around, taking his picture

Creevey, Dennis - Colin's younger brother; a Gryffindor [4]

Croaker - a member of the Department of Mysteries

Crockford, Doris - a woman Harry meets in his first trip to The Leaky Cauldron

Crouch Jr., Barty - sent to Azkaban by his own father

Dark Lord, The - see Voldemort

Delacour, Fleur - a student of Beauxbatons and a contestant in the Tri Wizard Tournament
Dueling Club demonstration

Ernie - driver of the Knight Bus

Figg, Mrs. - Dursley neighbor, Harry stayed every year with her on Dudley's birthday

Filch, Argus - Hogwarts caretaker

Finch-Fletchley, Justin - sorted into Hufflepuff

Finnigan, Seamus - sorted into Gryffindor; dad's a Muggle; mother is a witch

Flamel, Perenelle - Nicolas Flamel's wife
Flint, Marcus - captain of Slytherin Quidditch team
Fudge, Cornelius - Minister at the Ministry of Magic
Gordon - friend of Dudley
Goyle, Gregory - Draco Malfoy's friend
Gran - Neville's grandmother whom he lived with
Granger, Hermione [her-ME-own] - bushy-haired, buck-
    toothed, sassy and the smartest pupil at Hogwarts;
    Harry's friend in Gryffindor
Great Auntie Enid - Neville's ancestor
Great Uncle Algie - Neville's ancestor who tried to force magic out of him
Grunnion, Alberic - a wizard depicted on the Chocolate Frogs trading card series
Gudgeon, Davey - former Hogwarts student, nearly lost an eye touching
    the Whomping Willow
Gudgeon, Gladys - one of Lockhart's biggest fans
Hagrid, Rubeus [HAG-rid, roo-BAY-us] - the near-giant-sized Keeper of Keys and
    Grounds Keeper at Hogwarts. Hagrid is a former student of Hogwarts; was
    expelled in his third year
Hermione - see Granger, Hermione
He-who-must-not-be-named - another name for Lord Voldemort
Higgs, Terance - Seeker on the Slytherin Quidditch team
    during Harry's 1st year
Hopkirk, Mafalda - employee of the "improper Use of Magic" office at the
    Ministry of Magic
Johnson, Angelina - chaser on the Gryffindor Quidditch team
Jordan, Lee - friend and conspirator of the Weasley twins; he has dread locks
Kevin - toddler who uses his dad's wand to burst slugs
Krum, Viktor - player for Bulgarian Quidditch Team during the World Cup
Lockhart, Gilderoy - Defense Against the Dark Arts teacher in Harry's
    second year; author of self-glorifying autobiographies and five-time
    winner of Witch Weekly's "Most-Charming Smile Award"
Longbottom, Neville - forgetful and clumsy classmate of Harry's; a Gryffindor;
Lord Voldemort - see Voldemort
Lovegoods, - family that lives by the Weasleys, they attended the
    World Cup a week early
MacDougal, Morag - sorted into an unknown house

HAGRID

Macmillan, Ernie - Hufflepuff student and friend of Justin
Madam Rosmerta - see Rosmerta, Madam
Malcolm - friend of Dudley Dursley
Malfoy, Draco - a Slytherin, Harry's arch-enemy
Malfoy, Lucius - father of Draco Malfoy
Marge - see Aunt Marge
Mason - Mr. Dursley's biggest client
McGuffin, Jim - weatherman on Muggle television
Nott - student sorted into an unknown house at Hogwarts
Ogg - Game Keeper when Mrs. Weasley went to Hogwarts
Padfoot - the nickname of Sirius Black when a student at Hogwarts
Parkinson, Pansy - a Slytherin at Hogwarts

HERMIONE GRANGER

Patil, Padma - a Ravenclaw and twin of Parvati
Patil, Parvati - a Gryffindor and twin of Padma
Payne, Mr. - site manager of Diggory's campsite at the World Cup
Perks, Sally-Anne - student sorted into an unknown house at Hogwarts
Polkiss, Mrs. - Piers' mother
Polkiss, Piers - Dudley's best friend
Potter, Harry - an 11 year old boy who finds out his parents were wizards and is
    accepted into Hogwarts School of Witchcraft and Wizardry
Prang, Ernie - driver of the Knight Bus; "prang" means "to crash into"
Prewetts, The - one of four families killed by Voldemort
Professorhead - a name Peeves, the Poltergeist, calls Professor Dumbledore
Prongs - James Potter's nickname when he was a student at Hogwarts
Pucey, Adrian - chaser for the Slytherin Quidditch team
Riddle, Tom - father of Tom Marvolo Riddle
Roberts, Mr. - a Muggle and site manager of the Weasley's
    campsite at the World Cup
Rosmerta, Madam - the barmaid at The Three Broomsticks
Smethley, Veronica - Lockhart fan to whom Harry was addressing a
    letter when he heard the Basilisk's voice for the first time
snake - the mascot for Slytherin House
Spinnet, Alica - chaser for Gryffindor Quidditch team
Stan - conductor of the Knight Bus
Ted - newscaster on Muggle television
Thomas, Dean - a Gryffindor; a tall black boy and a fan of soccer
    who shares a room with Ron and Harry; he is a good artist

RON WEASLEY

Tom - bartender at The Leaky Cauldron

Turpin, Lisa - student sorted into Ravenclaw at Hogwarts

Uric the Oddball - mentioned in Binns' History of Magic class, a leader in the Goblin Rebellion

Weasley, Bill - was head boy at Hogwarts, a graduate and now works for Gringotts in Africa

Weasley, Charlie - was Quidditch captain at Hogwarts, somewhere in Romania studying dragons

Weasley, Fred - twin of George, Beater on Gryffindor Quidditch team

Weasley, George - twin of Fred, Beater on Gryffindor Quidditch team

Weasley, Ginny - youngest Weasley and the only girl, Ginny has a crush on Harry

Weasley, Molly - Weasley mother, wife of Arthur, very matronly and motherly

Weasley, Percy - a Gryffindor Prefect, currently the oldest Weasley student at Hogwarts

Weasley, Ron - youngest Weasley boy, Harry's best friend

Weatherby - a name Barty Crouch calls Percy

Wood, Oliver - captain of the Gryffindor Quidditch team

Wormtail - nickname given to Peter Pettigrew when a student at Hogwarts

You-know-who - the term given to Lord Voldemort when people are too afraid to say his name

Yvonne - Mrs. Dursley's friend, vacationing in Majorca

LORD VOLDEMORT
& LILLY POTTER

"Accio" - the Summoning Charm

Aconite - a plant used in potions which is also known as 'monkshood' or 'wolfsbane'

"Alohomora" - a spell to unlock a door

Animagi [an-im-AJ-eye] - wizards (plural) who are able to transform into an animal form.

"Aparecium" - a spell to make invisible ink appear

Apparate - the magical ability to disappear and re-appear at your destination

"Avada Kedavra" - The Killing Curse - one of the three unforgivable curses; a blinding green light that kills instantly

"Crucio" - Cruciatus Curse - one of the three unforgivable curses; a curse that provides the power to torture a creature or person by sheer will power

Curse of the Bogies - a spell Quirrell related to his students

Disapparation - a method by which experienced wizards travel; disappearing from one place and re-appearing in another

Dissendium - a spell which opened a secret passage inside a statue

Draught of Living Death -a powerful sleeping potion made of asphodel and wormwood

Elixer of Life - a liquid that has the power to make a wizard or witch live forever

Engorgio - Engorgement Charm - a spell which causes something to grow large

Ennervate - a spell to revive someone who has been stunned

"Expecto Patronum" - a spell to guard you from the Dementors by conjuring a patronus or patron

"Expelliarmus" - a disarming spell

"Ferula" - a spell to create a sling

Fidelius Charm - an extremely complex charm in which a secret is concealed within a single living soul

"Finite Incantatem" - a charm used by Snape to end commotion by students

Flame-Freezing Charm - used by ancient wizarding people (such as Wendelin the Weird) to freeze the flames meant to burn them

Floo Powder - a fine powder which allows wizards to travel from one place to another

Four Point Spell - a spell which enables your wand to point due North to reveal direction, discovered by Hermione

Furnunculus Curse - an unidentified curse used on Malfoy on the train home in Goblet of Fire

Homorphus Charm - a charm which turns a werewolf back into his human form

"Incendio" - a spell used to start a fire

Impediment Curse - a spell to slow down and obstruct attackers "Impedimenta"

"Impervious" - a magical spell Hermione places on Harry's glasses to repel water during a Quidditch match

"Imperio" - Impero Curse - one of the three unforgivable curses; a curse that allows you full control of another creature or person

Jelly-Legs Jinx - will cause your legs to wobble badly

"Locomoto mortis" - a spell for the leg-locker curse

"Lumos" - a charm to light the end of a wand (acts as a flashlight)

Memory Charm - effects memory - used on Muggles to erase their memory of wizarding experiences

Mobiliarbus - the magical way of moving objects

Mobilicorpus - when a person can't walk on his own, this magic makes it seem as if invisible strings are holding the person up

Muggle Repelling Charms - charms which prevent Muggles from stumbling into an unwanted area

"Nox" - a charm used to turn out the light on your wand after you say "lumos"

"Obliviate" - a memory modifying charm

Patronus - an anti-dementor created by using the spell

PROFESSOR SPROUT

"Expecto Patronum" - while thinking happy thoughts "patronus totalus"

"Peskipiksi Pesternomi" - a spell used by Lockhart to get rid of destructive Cornish pixies (it doesn't work)

"Petrificus Totalus" - a spell for the Full Body-Bind, causing the subject to lie motionless (petrified)

Polyjuice Potion - a potion that makes a person change into a different person

Portkey - an object which is "used to transport wizards from one spot to another at a prearranged time"

Potions - a class at Hogwarts taught by Severus Snape. Potions class teaches students how to make potions such as enlarging potions, bubbling potions, etc.

"Priori Incantato" - a spell which, when placed on a wand, causes the wand to identify the most recent spell that it performed

Priori Incantatem - an effect which occurs when two wands of the same core material are brought into combat with one another, causing one to force the other to release shades of former spells. This effect is characterized by the appearance of bright, gold-colored threads which unite the two wands and encase their owners

"Reducio" - a spell to reduce objects in size

"Reducto" - Reductor Curse - blasts and moves objects away

"Rictusempra" - a tickling charm

CHARMS, SPELLS, POTIONS, CURSES

"Ridikulus" - a charm to make a Boggart take on characteristics of a person or object which the one using the charm is thinking of

"Serpensortia" - a charm used to summon snakes

Shrivelfig - an ingredient in magic potions, used in Shrinking Solution

Skele-Gro - a type of medicinal potion used to cure de-boneing When a person takes Skele-Gro, the bones grow back, but it's painful

Sonorus - A charm that allows your voice to be amplified

Stupify - A spell used to stop or hold

Summoning Charm - created with the spell, "Accio"

Swelling Solution - it causes swelling when it touches a person

"Tarantallegra" - a dancing spell

Transfiguration - a spell which changes the nature of a person or object completely - - the molecular structure of the object is altered

Veritaserum - a truth potion

"Waddiwasi" - a spell used by Prof. Lupin to send gum up Peeve's nose

"Wingardium Leviosa" - a spell to make things fly

Wolfsbane Potion - a potion which makes a werewolf safe during the full moon

Wormwood - an herb which, when combined with ashphodel, makes a sleeping potion so powerful it's known as the "drought of living death"

THE WEASLEY
FLYING FORD ANGELICA

Aragog - a huge spider in the forbidden forest

Animagus [an-im-AJ-us] - a wizard who is able to transform into an animal form

Badger - mascot for Hufflepuff

Bane - a centaur in the Forbidden Forest; black haired and bodied

Basilisk - the King of Serpents; anyone who is fixed with the beam of this giant snake's eyes dies instantly

Binkey - Lavendar Brown's pet rabbit

Blast-Ended Skrewt - a magical creature that can burn, sting and bite all at once in addition to suck blood

NORBERT

boarhound - the type of dog that Hagrid has (Fang)

Boa Constrictor - a snake at the zoo; Harry "talks" to in parsel tongue

Brandon Banshee - a banshee banished by a hair-lipped witch

Bubotubers - a thick, black, giant slug-like plant that must be squeezed to collect pus used for magical charms and spells

Buckbeak - a Hippogriff (a beast which is half horse and half eagle)

Centaur - a mythical creature that is half-horse and half man. It has the body and legs of a horse; the arms and face of a man

Chameleon Ghouls - a creature that can disguise itself as something else

Common Welsh Green - a breed of wild dragon found in Britain

Cornish Pixies - devilish little fairies that wreak havoc

Crookshanks - Hermione's cat

Dementor - a creature who feeds on the happy emotions of humans, leaving one cold and sad. The Dementor sucks the very soul out of a human, leaving him emotionless

Dementor's Kiss - see Kiss of a Dementor

Devil's Snare - a plant which entraps anyone whom it can reach

Dobby - Malfoy's house elf

Eagle - the mascot for Ravenclaw house

Errol - the Weasley family owl

Elves - small creatures living in the Forbidden Forest where they hold midnight feasts and play pranks

Fang - Hagrid's pet boarhound

Fawkes - Dumbledore's Phoenix (a bird which dies and is reborn again)

Firenze - [FEER-en-zay] a centaur in the Forbidden Forest, young with white-blonde hair and a palomino body

Flesh-Eating Slugs - pests which infested the Hogwarts cabbages

Flobberworm - a harmless, worm-like magical creature which students must keep alive in order to pass Care of Magical Creatures class

Fluffy - a huge three headed dog protecting a secret chamber at Hogwarts

Gillyweed - gnome - see also de-gnome, a small creature which wreaks havoc in Wizard gardens and must be removed

Goblins - creatures that run Gringotts, the wizard bank

Grim - a giant black dog seen as a death omen; when someone sees a Grim, it is believed that he/she will soon die

Griphook - a goblin at Gringotts

Grindylow - a water demon

Hebridean Black - a breed of wild dragon found in Britain

Hedwig - Harry's snowy owl, a gift from Hagrid

Hermes - Percy Weasley's owl

Hedwig

Hinkypunk - a creature with a lantern; on dark nights it leads lost people into bogs and swamps

Hippogriff - a magical creature which has the head and talons of an eagle and the back, hind legs and tail of a horse

Horntail - a type of dragon

House Elves - small creatures which work as servants in some wizard homes; they can only be set free when the master offers the elf a piece of clothing

Kappa - water-dwellers - they look like scaly monkeys with webbed hands; they strangle those who wade into their ponds

Leprechauns - Ireland's team mascots; little green magical people that carry a minute lamp of gold or green

Lion - the mascot for Gryffindor

Mandrake - a plant which has a screaming baby on the end, the cry is fatal to all who hear it. A mandrake plant, when full-grown, is a powerful restorative used to return those who have been transfigured back to their original state

Merpeople - mermaids and mermen who live at the bottom of the lake in the forbidden forest

Mr. Paws - one of Mrs. Figg's cats

Mrs. Norris - Filch's scrawny cat who spies on the students and reports to Filch

DEMENTORS

Morsmodre - a summoning spell to conjure up the Dark Mark

Mosag - Aragog's wife

Nagini - a giant snake at least 12 feet long whose milk helps sustain Voldemort

Norbert - a Norwegian Ridgeback dragon that Hagrid hatches after he wins the egg at a pub

Norwegian Ridgeback - a rare type of dragon (see Norbert)

Peeves - the Hogwarts poltergeist who is always up to mischief and pranks

Phoenix - Dumbledore's pet bird; its tears can heal wounds

Pigwidgeon (or Pig) - a small owl given to Ron by Sirius Black

Red Cap - a creature that lives wherever there is bloodshed

Ripper - Aunt Marge's precious bull hound

Ronan - a centaur in the Forbidden Forest (see centaur)

Scabbers - Ron's hand-me-down rat; fat, old and useless

Scops Owl - a breed of owl, very small and used for "Local Deliveries Only"s

Snake - the mascot for Slytherin

Snowy - one of Ms. Figg's cats with which she bores Harry

Stupefy - A spell to freeze and render motionless

Trevor - Neville's pet toad who is always escaping from his owner

Troll - a creature who lives in the forest and under bridges and can be dangerous

Tuffy - one of Ms. Figg's cats with which she bores Harry

Tibbles - one of Ms. Figg's cats with which she bores Harry

Trevor - Neville's pet toad who is always escaping from his owner

Unicorn - a horse-like creature with a horn coming out of its head. If you are near death and you drink its silvery blood, it will keep you alive for a limited time...at a price: you will be cursed and half of your life will be taken away. It is faster than a werewolf and very graceful. Its hair is used in Potions

Veela - Bulgarian team mascots that have the ability to lure the viewer's mind into wanting them

Werewolf - a creature that is half wolf and half man

Whizzing Worms - magical worms used in potions and spells

Whomping Willow - a tree outside Hogwarts that becomes violent against anything it comes in contact with

Winky - Barty Crouch's house elf who comes to work at Hogwarts

THE WHOMPING WILLOW

GHOSTS

NEARLY
HEADLESS NICK

Binns, Prof - a ghost who teaches History of Magic at Hogwarts

Bloody Baron, The - the ghost of the Slytherin Tower. Not much is known about him other than he is very wicked and scary looking; his eyes are blank, black sockets and his robes are covered in silver blood. He is the only "person" who can control Peeves the Poltergeist

Cadogan, Sir - slightly demented knight that inhabits a painting on the landing of the seventh floor in Hogwarts. Temporary guardian of Gryffindor Tower

De Mimsy-Porpington, Sir Nicholas - another name for **Nearly-Headless Nick** - resident ghost of Gryffindor

Delaney-Podmore, Patrick - leader of the Headless Hunt

Fat Friar, The - resident ghost of Hufflepuff

Fat Lady, The - woman in a pink silk dress who sits in a portrait and protects the entrance to Gryffindor

Grey Lady, The - the ghost of Ravenclaw, named in Book 4. "Hundreds of years ago an earl, John Dudley, tried to take over the English throne with his accomplice, Lady Jane Grey. They were beheaded, and Lady Jane's ghost is still said to be walking around Dudley Castle. Her nickname has been for the past several decades, The Grey Lady ghost

Moaning Myrtle - a ghost who haunts the toilet in the girl's bathroom. She moans loudly and complains that no one likes her (which is probably true)

Nearly Headless Nick - resident ghost of Gryffindor

Peeves - the Hogwarts poltergeist that causes havoc and pranks in the castle; can only be controlled by The Bloody Baron

Abyssinian Shrivelfigs - plants in the Herbology class

Accidental Magic Reversal Squad - a team of rescuers from the Ministry of Magic, also known as Obliviators

Animagi [an-im-AJ-eye] - wizards (plural) with the ability to transform into an animal form

Apparate - magical travel enabling one to disappear and appear in another location

Arithmancy - a class taken by Hermione; the study of numbers

Astronomy - a class at Hogwarts for the study of the galaxy, planets and stars

Auror - a witch or wizard that tracks down Death Eaters and other bad/dark wizards; takes them to Azkaban - the wizard prison

Beater - a position on Quidditch team

Beauxbatons - a school of witchcraft and wizardry in France

Beauxbaton carriage - a means by which Beauxbaton students arrive at Hogwarts, pulled by a dozen winged palomino

Bertie Bott's Every Flavor Beans - a wizard candy coming in every flavor, such as chocolate,   peppermint, spinach, liver, tripe and vomit

Bezoar - a stone taken from the stomach of a goat which will save a person from poisons

Blood-Flavoured Lollipops - treats for vampires

Bludger - a jet black Quidditch ball, slightly smaller than a soccer ball; can cause serious injury during the game

Bode - a member of the Department of Mysteries

Boggart - a shape shifter which takes on the likeness of one's worst fear

Bones, The - one of the 4 family killed by Voldemort

Boot - a Portkey (see Portkey) on Stoatshead Hill used to apparate **Broom** - a long handled implement made of twigs which witches and wizards use for flying

Broomstick Servicing Kit - a kit containing helpful items to keep a broom in mint condition

Butterbeer - a frothy, buttery hot drink served in Hogsmeade (a favorite of Hermione and Ron)

"Caput Draconis" - a password for Gryffindor tower

Care of Magical Creatures - a class taught by Hagrid

Catchpole - a village near the Weasley family home

Cauldron - a pot for making potions

Cauldron Cakes - a treat on the Hogwarts Express cart

Charm - a magical spell

Chaser - a position on Quidditch team

Chipolata - a type of long, skinny sausage served during the Christmas feast

Chocoballs - a chocolate sweet sold in Honeydukes

Chocolate Frogs - a favorite wizard candy that comes with Famous Wizards Cards

Chudley Cannons, The - a professional Quidditch team Ron admires at the Quidditch Cup Finals

Circe [SIR-see] - a witch depicted on the Chocolate Frogs trading card series; a figure from Greek mythology known for turning men into pigs

Cleansweep Seven - a respected type of broomstick for flying

Cliodna - a druidess depicted on the Chocolate Frogs trading card series

Cockroach Clusters - a rather nasty sweet made of cockroaches sold in Honeydukes

Comet Two-Sixty - the top-of-the-line broom Draco Malfoy first owns

Committee for the Disposal of Dangerous Creatures - an office at the Ministry of Magic protecting against fierce animals

Committee on Experimental Charms - an office at the Ministry of Magic

Croaker - a member of the Department of Mysteries

Daily Mail - the Muggle newspaper

Daily Prophet - Wizards' newspaper

Daisy Root - an ingredient used in a shrinking solution

Dark Arts - the practice of evil spells, curses, potions, charms and the use of dark mythical creatures

Dark Lord, The - another name for Lord Voldemort

Dark Mark, The - the sign of Voldemort

Death Eaters - supporters of Voldemort

THE DARK MARK

Deathday Party - a party celebrated by a ghost on the anniversary of his/her death

Decree for the Restriction of Underage Wizadary - a law prohibiting Hogwarts students from using magic while not at school

De-gnoming - the art of removing pesky garden gnomes

Department of Mysteries - a top secret department at the Ministry of Magic, members are known as "unspeakables"

Diddy - a pet name for Dudley from his mother

Dis-apparate - the means to leave and disappear

Divination - a fortune-telling class

Dr. Filibuster's Fabulous Wet-Start, No-Heat Fireworks - the Weasley twins favorite; they explode with red & blue stars that bounce around a room for at least 30 minutes

Dot - a customer at The Hanged Man pub

"Draco Dormiens Nunquam Titillandus" - Hogwarts motto,
"Never Tickle a Sleeping Dragon"

Drooble's Best Blowing Gum - a wizard chewing gum

Dueling Club - a club started in Hogwarts to teach about wizard duels

Dungbombs - a trick item you can buy at Zonko's

Elfric the Eager - a subject in History of Magic

Elves - small creatures which live deep in the Forbidden Forest where
they hold midnight feasts and play pranks on the lost passerby

Emeric the Evil - mentioned in Binns' History of Magic class

Erised - see Mirror of Erised

Every Flavor Beans - see Bertie Bott's Every Flavor Beans

Exploding Bonbons - a treat found in the Hogsmede store, in Honeydukes

Exploding Snap - a game played by wizards

Famous Wizard Cards - trading cards of famous wizards through the ages; packaged
with Chocolate Frogs

Fawcetts, The - a wizard family that couldn't get tickets for the World Cup

Filibuster Fireworks - Dr. Filibuster's Fabulous Wet-Start, No-Heat Fireworks

Firebolt - a top-of-the-line broom given to Harry as a gift from an unknown friend

Fizzing Whizbees - levitating sherbert balls

Flibber Gibbet - one of the passwords for Gryffindor house

Flying Carpets - technically defined as Muggle artifacts although argued to be a
family vehicle

Foe-Glass - the glass on the wall where Dumbledore appeared before saving Harry

Ford Anglia - the Weasley flying magical family car

Goblin Liason Office - an office at the Ministry of Magic

Gobstones - a marbles-like Wizard game where the pieces squirt a stinky substance

Golden Snitch (or Snitch) - a golden Quidditch ball about the size of a large walnut
with tiny silver wings

Great Humberto, The - a television show airing Monday nights which Dudley enjoys

Gregory the Smarmy - a statue at Hogwarts

Grunnings - the drill company run by Harry's Uncle Vernon

Half-blood - a witch or wizard who has one wizard parent and one Muggle parent

Hand of Glory - a withered hand on a cushion which, when a candle is inserted,
gives light only to the person holding it

MIRROR OF ESRID

"Harry Hunting" - a favorite game of Dudley and his friends

Head Boy/Head Girl - an honored 7th-year student at Hogwarts; a school-wide honor with only one head boy and one head girl selected

Headless Hunt - an exclusive membership of headless huntsmen ghosts who participate in hunt activities

Heir of Slytherin - the true heir of one of the founders of Hogswarts

Herbology - the study of plants and mythical plants

"His Eyes Are as Green As a fresh Pickled Toad" - a poem written by Ginny Weasley to Harry on Valentine's Day

Hog's Head, The - the pub in the village where Hagrid won a dragon's egg

Hogwarts Express - a train which takes students from London

House Championship - a yearly contest between the four houses of Hogwarts

House Cup - a trophy awarded to the House with the most points at the end of the year

House Points - points awarded to or taken from a house depending on the actions of its members

Howler - a letter which yells messages and burns up after being opened

Hufflepuff - a Hogwarts house named for one of the founders, Helga Hufflepuff

Hut-on-the-Rock - a place Uncle Vernon takes the family to hide from Hagrid

Ice Mice - the gum that makes your teeth squeak and chatter

Ickle Duddeykins - a "baby-talk" name Mrs. Dursley uses to dote on Dudley

"Ickle Firsties" - a name Peeves uses to mock first year students; "little first years"

Invisibility Booster - a device installed in Mr. Weasley's car to make it invisible

Invisibility Cloak - a shiny, silvery grey cloth which makes everything it covers invisible

Jelly Slugs - a sweet sold in Honeydukes

Jigger, Arsenius - wrote Magical Drafts and Potions Johnson

Keeper - position on Quidditch team, protector of goal

Kip - slang for "nap" or "sleep"

Knickerbocker Glory - an English ice cream dessert

Knight Bus - a bus which can be called upon by wizards in distress; summoned by raising the wand arm

Knockturn Alley - a side street in Diagon Alley; shops featuring the dark arts

Knuts - little bronze coins, wizard currency; 29 Knutes to a Sickle

Kwikspell - correspondence course in beginner's magic

Leaky Cauldron, The - an old pub and inn in London and secret entrance to Diagon Alley

Lemon Drops or Sherbet Lemons - Dumbledore's favorite muggle candy

SIRIUS BLACK

McKinnons, The - one of four families killed by Voldemort

Medal for Magical Merit - an award given to Tom Riddle when he was Head Boy

Mega-Mutilation - Part Three - Dudley's Play Station game

Ministry of Magic - in charge of keeping witches and wizards secret from Muggles

Mirror of Erised - a magical mirror that shows not your face, but your heart's desire

Monkshood - a plant used in potions which is the same as wolfsbane a.k.a. "Anacote"

Moon - a student sorted into an unknown house at Hogwarts

Moony - the nickname of Remus Lupin as a student at Hogwarts

"Muggle" - a wizard term for non-magic folk

Muggle Protection Act - a law that prevents people of the magical community from using magic in a way that Muggles can see

Muggle Studies - a class to study Muggles

"Never Tickle a Sleeping Dragon" - Hogwarts School Motto

N.E.W.T. - the abbreviation of Nastily Exhausting Wizarding Tests

Nimbus 2000 - a well-respected type of broomstick for flying

Nimbus 2001 - an upgrade on the Nimbus 2000

Obliviators - members of the Accidental Magic Reversal Squad

CORNELIUS FUDGE

Omnioculars - magical binoculars which allow instant replay, slow-motion , etc.

One-Eyed Witch - a statue containing a secret passage to Honeyduke's village

O.W.L.s (Ordinary Wizarding Levels) - a test taken at the end of the 5th year by students at Hogwarts

Owl Post -the magic community postal service

Owls - birds used by the magical community to carry their mail called "Owl Post"

Parselmouth - a wizard who has the ability to speak to snakes; believed to be the mark of a Dark Wizard

Parseltongue - the name of the language spoken by a parselmouth

Pepper Imps - a candy that makes you breath fire

Philosopher's Stone a.k.a. Sorcerer's Stone - a substance which turns any metal into gold; produces the Elixir of Life which will make the drinker immortal

Pocket Sneakoscope - a small spinning glass top that lights up; makes a high-pitched whistle when is somebody or something is suspicious

Portkey - can be any object which is magically charmed; used to transport wizards from one spot to another at prearranged times

Potions - a class at Hogwarts taught by Severus Snape

Prefect - an honor student at Hogwarts

Prewetts, The - one of four families killed by Voldemort

Professorhead - a name Peeves calls Dumbledore

Puddlemere United - a professional Quidditch team

Pumpkin Juice - a beverage enjoyed by wizards and witches

Pumpkin Pasties [PASS-teez] - a treat on the Hogwarts Express cart

Pure-blood - slang term for wizards born of two wizarding families

"Pure-blood" - the password to the Slytherin common room

Put-Outer - a device used to turn street lamps on and off

Quaffle - bright red Quidditch ball; the size of a soccer ball

Quality Quidditch Supplies - a shop in Diagon Alley which sells broom sticks and other Quidditch supplies

Quidditch - a wizard sport played in the air on broomsticks

Quidditch Cup - a trophy given to the champion Quidditch team at the end of a season

Quidditch Season - begins in November ends in Spring

Quidditch World Cup - the International Quidditch tournament

PROFESSOR SNAPE

Registry of Proscribed Charmable Objects - determines items that can be charmed

Remembrall - a glass marble-sized ball which, when held, turns red to tell the holder if they've forgotten something

St. Brutis's Secure Center for Incurably Criminal Boys - how the Dursley's explained Harry's absences during the school year

Salem Witches' Institute - a group of American witches attending the Quidditch World Cup

"Draco Dormiens Nunquam Titillandus" - "Never Tickle a Sleeping Dragon"

Secret-keeper - a person entrusted with another's secret

Seeker - Quidditch position for catching the Golden Snitch

Sherbert Balls - a candy bought at Honeydukes in Hogsmeade; when sucking on them you levitate a couple inches from the ground

Shooting Star - an outdated flying broomstick

Sickles - silver coins, wizard currency; 17 Sickles to a Galleon

Smeltings stick - stick used at Smeltings on 1st year students as a school tradition

Snitch (or Golden Snitch) - in Quidditch, a flying gold ball with silver wings; earns 150 points for the seeker who catches it

Sorcerer's Stone - a substance which turns any metal into gold; produces the Elixir of Life which will make the drinker immortal

Sorting Ceremony - a ceremony where First Year students are placed into one of 4 Hogwarts houses

Sorting Hat, The - an old wizard's hat which assigns new students to their houses at Hogwarts

Special Award for Services to the School - a plaque given to Tom Riddle showing he was once a good person

Spell-O-Tape - unpredictable wizards tape, used to mend broken items

S.P.E.W. - the organization founded by Hermione to stop abuse of house elves at Hogwarts

Splinched - when a wizard Apparates improperly and leaves half of himself behind

Squib - a child of two wizards who shows no wizarding ability

Stink Pellets - small items when thrown, explode, releasing fumes that smell very unpleasant; sold at Zonko's joke shop in Hogsmeade

Time-turner - a necklace with an hourglass on it which enables the user to go back in time

Toad Peppermint Creams - a wizard candy sold at Hogsmeades

Ton-Tongue Toffee - candy which causes the tongue to grow huge and heavy and flop out of your mouth

Toothflossing Stringmints - keeps your teeth clean

Transfiguration - a class at Hogwarts taught by Professor McGongall

Treacle Tarts - a bread crumb, lemon tart pie

Triwizard Tournament - the 100 year old competition between the three largest Wizarding schools, a school champion competes in a series of three challenging / dangerous tasks

Twig Trimmer - a device used to cut splintered twigs from your broom

Wand - for magic (willow is good for charm work, mahogany for transfiguration)

"Wattlebird" - the Gryffindor password

Weasley's Wizard Wheezes - a product line of joke items invented by the Weasley twins (Fred & George)

Which Broomstick - a book or catalogue which describes the different makes of flying broomsticks complete with mail order

Wimbourne Wasps - a Quidditch team, Ludo Bagman was a star Beater in his day

Witches Weekly - a magazine for witches which has a contest for most charming smile

Witching Hour - a wizard radio program

Wizard Chess - a game of chess with giant, living pieces

Wizard's Duel - a one-on-one fight between wizard's; a challenge with wands

Wolfsbane - a plant used in potions; same as monkshood; also goes by the name of "aconite"

Wormwood - an herb used in sleeping potions so powerful it's known as the "drought of living death"

#4 Privet Drive - the home of the Dursleys. (Harry's Aunt Petunia, Uncle Vernon and his cousin Dudley) Harry has lived here from age 1 to age 10 in a cupboard in the closet

7th Floor - the entrance to the Gryffindor common room

Africa - (Egypt) country where Bill Weasley works for Gringotts

Azkaban - a magical wizard prison where dark wizards and criminals of the magic world are kept. Guarded day and night by the terrifying Dementors, who can drain peace, hope and happiness out of any human who comes too close to them

Black Forest - a place in Germany where Professor Quirrell was rumored to have encountered vampires

Borgin and Burkes - the Dark Arts shop in Knockturn Alley

Burrow, The - the name of the Weasley home

Chamber of Secrets - a secret chamber somewhere in Hogwarts created by Salazar Slytherin which was the home of a horrible beast that would be unleashed by the heir of Slytherin to rid the school of Muggles

Common Room - the meeting room for each Hogwarts house

Dervish and Banges - the wizarding equipment store in Hogsmeade

Diagon Alley - a long cobbled street filled with the most fascinating wizarding shops in the world. Accessible through the Leaky Cauldron pub in London.

Eeylops Owl Emporium - a shop in Diagon Alley where Harry picked out his owl, Hedwig

Eton - a school for Muggles

Florean Fortescue's Ice-Cream Parlor - a shop in Diagon Alley

Florish and Botts - a school books shop in Diagon Alley

Forbidden Forest The - the forest that surrounds the Hogwarts Castle and grounds. Hagrid lives on the edge of the forest. It provides a protection to Hogwarts in addition to a place where many magical creatures reside

Great Hall, The - the main gathering and meal hall for all Hogwarts students; where the Sorting Hat ceremony is held for first year students. The ceiling is bewitched to look like the sky.

Great Hangleton - the neighboring town of Little Hangleton

Godric Hollow - the place where Lily and James Potter lived

Gringotts - the Wizard bank run by Goblins and located hundreds of miles under Diagon Alley in London

Grunnings - Uncle Vernon's Drill Business

Gryffindor, Hufflepuff, Ravenclaw, Slytherin - the four houses in Hogwarts are named after each of the four great wizards; Godric Gryffindor, Helga Hufflepuff, Rowena Ravenclaw, and Salazar Slytherin (who turned to the Dark Arts); the dormitories are located in four different towers

Gryffindor House - located on the 7th floor and named after Cedric Gryffindor, one of the four original founding wizards of Hogwarts. The colors are Red & Gold and the mascot is the Lion. Professor McGonagall is the Deputy Head Mistress at Hogwarts and also serves as head of Gryffindor House. Harry, Hermione and the Weasleys are the main characters who reside in Gryffindor

Hanged Man, The - the village pub of Little Hangleton

High Table, The - the faculty table in the Great Hall where Dumbledore presides

Hog's Head, The - a pub in the village where Hagrid won a dragon's egg

Hogsmeade - a secret and completely magical village in Britain. Hogsmeade is not far from Hogwarts and has an array of wonderful shops including Honeydukes sweet shop, the Three Broomsticks pub and Zonko's joke shop

Hogsmeade Station - Hogwarts Express stops here to drop off the students each year

Hogwarts School of Witchcraft and Wizardry - a magical school for wizard students ages 11-17; located somewhere in Scotland and quite special; the rooms, dungeons and floors are constantly changing (See special page - Hogwarts Castle)

Honeydukes - the wizarding sweet shop in Hogsmeade

House - one of four dormitories the students are assigned to upon arriving in their first year, placed there by the Sorting Hat

Hufflepuff House - located in Hufflepuff Tower; is named after Helga Hufflepuff, one of the four original founding wizards of Hogwarts; the mascot is the Badger

Kings Cross Train Station - the train station where the bright red shuttle train, The Hogwarts Express, takes off every year on September 1st

Knockturn Alley - a street of wizard shops devoted totally to the Dark Arts

Leaky Cauldron, The - a pub and secret entrance to Diagon Alley

Madam Malkin's - a shop in Diagon Alley selling wizarding robes for all occasions

Ministry of Magic -the agency that tries to keep witches and wizards secret from the Muggles

Ollivander's Wand Shop - a Diagon Alley shop where Harry purchased his wand

Platform Nine and Three Quarters - the hidden platform which can only be accessed by walking through a concrete barrier between Platform Nine and Platform Ten

Ravenclaw House - located in Ravenclaw Tower, and is named after Rowena Ravenclaw; the mascot is the Eagle

Riddle House, The - the home of the Riddle family in the village of Little Hangleton

Romania - a country where Charlie Weasley is studying dragons

Shrieking Shack - by pushing a knob on the Whomping Willow you may safely pass to the Shrieking Shack

Slytherin House - one of the school houses in Hogwarts. Founded by Salazar Slytherin. The Slytherin symbol is a snake. The resident ghost is the Bloody Baron. Harry's arch-enemy, Draco Malfoy, is in Slytherin. Professor Snape is head of Slytherin house.

Smeltings - Dudley Dursley's private school. Uncle Vernon's alma mater

Stoatshead Hill - location of the Portkey for traveling to the Quidditch World Cup Match

St. Mungo's Hospital for Magical Maladies and Injuries - where Frank Longbottom and his wife (Neville's parents) are committed as "insane"

The Burrow - where the Weasleys live

The Whomping Willow - a magical tree in the Forbidden Forest at Hogwarts that protects a secret passage to the Shrieking Shack in Hogsmeade

Three Broomsticks, The - a pub in Hogsmeade

Vauxhall Road, London - the location of a Muggle variety store

Zonko's - a wizard joke shop in Hogsmeade

OWL POST

Adventures of Martin Miggs, the Mad Muggle, The - a comic book Ron owns

A Beginners' Guide to Transfiguration - authored by Switch, Emeric

A Guide to Medieval Sorcery - author unknown

A History of Magic - author Bagshot, Bathilda

An Anthology of Eighteenth Century Charms - author unknown

Beginner's Guide to Transfiguration - one of Ginny Weasley's books

Break With A Banshee - a book by Gilderoy Lockhart that is required for all 2nd years

Charm Your Own Cheese - Book at the Weasley's home

Common Magical Ailments and Afflictions - a standard health book for magic people

Daily Prophet - the wizards' newspaper

Death Omens: What To Do When You Know The Worst Is Coming book on death
omens

Dreadful Denizens of the Deep - author unknown

Enchantment in Baking - a book at the Weasley home

Encyclopedia of Toadstools - a book that Lucius Malfoy gets hit with

Fantastic Beasts and Where to Find Them - authored by Newt Scamander

Flying with the Cannons - a book Harry reads the summer before his 4th year

Gadding With Ghouls - authored by Gilderoy Lockhart

Gilderoy Lockhart's Guide to Household Pests - removing pesky garden gnomes

Handbook of Do-It Yourself Broomcare - a book Hermione gives to Harry

Hogwarts, a History - a book about Hogwarts

Holidays With Hags - a book by Gilderoy Lockhart

Intermediate Transfiguration - author unknown

Invisible Book of Invisibility, The - available at the bookshop-Diagon Alley-if you can find it

Madcap Magic for Wacky Warlocks - author unknown

Magical Droughts and Potions - a book by Arsenius Jigger

Magical Me - autobiography of Gilderoy Lockhart

Magical Theory and **A History Of Magic -** by Waffling, A. Dalbert

Magical Water Plants of the Mediterranean - author unknown, book given to
　　　Neville by Professor Moody
Modern Magical History - a book about the history of the magical world
Monster Book of Monsters, The - a textbook chosen by Hagrid for the Care
　　　of Magical Creatures course for third-years. It will bite and run away
　　　from one unless it is stroked down the spine
Moste Potente Potions - a book in the restricted section of the Hogwarts library
Old and Forgotten Bewitchments and Charms - author unknown
One Minute Feasts- It's Magic - a book at the Weasley home
One Thousand Magical Herbs and Fungi - Phyllida Spore
**Powers You Never Knew you Had and What to Do with Them Now You've
Wised Up** - unknown author
**Predicting the Unpredictable: Insulate Yourself Against Shocks and Broken Ball:
When Fortunes Turn Fowl** - unknown author
Prefects Who Gained Power - a book which interests Percy in
　　　a junk shop in Diagon Alley
Saucy Tricks for Tricky Sorts - author unknown
Sites of Historical Sorcery - a book, quoted as saying that the inn at Hogsmeade was
　　　the headquarters for the 1612 goblin rebellion, and
　　　that the Shrieking Shack is the most severely haunted building in Britain
Sonnets of a Sorcerer - a cursed book, everyone who read from it spoke in limericks
for the rest of their lives
Standard Book of Spells - by Goshawk, Miranda - required text at Hogwarts
　　　("Grade" indicates year - "The Standard Book of Spells, Grade One"
　　　was required for first year students, "Grade Two" for second
　　　year, and so on)
Travels With Trolls - a book by Gilderoy Lockhart
The Dark Forces: A Guide to Self-Protection - by Quintin Trimble
The Rise and Fall of the Dark Arts - author unknown
Unfogging The Future - book by Cassandra Vablatsky
Viridian, Vindictus Curses and Countercurse - Bewitch your friends and befuddle
　　　your enemies with the latest revenges: hair loss, jelly-legs, tongue-tying , etc.
Voyages With Vampires - a book by Gilderoy Lockhart
Wanderings With Werewolves - a book by Gilderoy Lockhart
Weird Wizarding Dilemmas and Their Solutions - author unknown
Year With The Yeti - a book by Gilderoy Lockhart

Agrippa - a wizard depicted on the Chocolate Frogs trading card series

Archie - an old wizard who passes as a Muggle by wearing a long flowery nightgown

Auror - a witch or wizard that hunts Death Eaters and other bad/dark wizards; for internment in Azkaban Prison

Azkaban - the wizard prison

Bagman, Ludo - head of the Department of Magical Games and Sports; accused of being a Death Eater by Karkaroff

Bagman, Otto - brother of Ludo Bagman

Bashir, Ali - a wizard who was angry about the embargo on flying carpets

Basil - a wizard wearing a muggle "kilt" at the World Cup

Black, Sirius - James Potter's best friend at Hogwarts; Harry's godfather; sent to Azkaban on murder charges

Circe [SIR-see] - a wizard depicted on the Chocolate Frogs trading card series

Crouch, Barty - works for the ministry of magic; he put his son, Barty Jr., in Azkaban

Diggle, Dedalus - wizard who made shooting stars fly over the city of Kent, meets Harry in Diagon Alley

Diggory, Amos - Cedric Diggory's father

Dippet, Prof. - the headmaster when Tom Riddle attended Hogwarts

Dolohov Antonin - an accused Death Eater as attested by Karkaroff at his trial

Dumbledore, Aberforth - the brother of Albus Dumbledore, once prosecuted for practicing inappropriate charms on a goat

Dumbledore, Albus - the current headmaster of Hogwarts; he has a long silvery beard, a very crooked nose and half moon spectacles

Fawcetts, The - a wizard family that couldn't get tickets for the World Cup

Filch, Argus - the caretaker and staff member at Hogwarts

Flamel, Nicolas - an alchemist and friend of Dumbledore

Flamel, Perenelle - the wife of Nicolas Flamel

Flitwick, Professor - a charms teacher at Hogwarts

Fudge, Cornelius - the Minister at the Ministry of Magic

Grindelwald - a Dark Wizard defeated by Dumbledore in 1945

Gryffindor, Godric - the founder of Gryffindor House at Hogwarts

Hengist of Woodcroft - a wizard depicted on the Chocolate Frogs trading card series

Hooch, Madam - teaches broomstick flying at Hogwarts

Karkaroff, Igor - Headmaster of the Durmstrang school

Kettleburn, Prof. - taught Care of Magical Creatures prior to Hagrid

Lockhart, Gilderoy - the Defense Against the Dark Arts teacher in Harry's second year; author of self-glorifying autobiographies

PROFESSOR
LOCKHART

Longbottom Frank - Neville's father, an auror, driven insane after being tortured by Voldemort; committed to a sanitarium

Lupin, Remus J. - the Defense Against the Dark Arts teacher in Harry's third year

Madam Maxine - the headmistress of Beauxbaton School; a competing school in the Tri-Wizard Tournament (GOF)

Malfoy, Lucius - Draco Malfoy's father

McGonagall, Minerva - the Deputy Headmistress of Hogwarts, and head of Gryffindor

McKinnons, The one of four families killed by Voldemort

Merlin - a wizard depicted on the Chocolate Frogs trading card series, traditionally thought to have trained King Arthur

Mockridge, Cuthbert - the head of the Goblin Liaison Office

Moody, Mad-Eye - Harry's 4th year Defense Against the Dark Arts teacher and retired Aurer (Dark Arts hunter)

"MAD EYE" MOODY

Morgana - a witch depicted on the Chocolate Frogs trading card series, believed to be the half-sister of King Arthur

Mortlake - professor of Transfiguration at Hogwarts; was questioned about "extremely odd ferrets" by Committee on Experimental Charms

Paracelsus - a wizard depicted on the Chocolate Frogs trading card series

Peasegood, Arnold - a member of the Accidental Magic Reversal Squad

Perkins - co-worker of Mr. Weasley's; suffers from lumbago

Pettigrew - a wizard who was a friend of James Potter in his school days and later became known as "Wormtail", betrayed James to Voldemort

Pince, Madam - the Hogwarts School Librarian

Pomfrey, Poppy - the stern school nurse at Hogwarts

Pontner, Roddy - a wizard who bets on the Quidditch World Cup game

Potter, James - Harry's father, a pure-blooded wizard

Potter, Lily - Harry's Muggle mother who died protecting him from Lord Voldemort

Prewetts, The - one of four families killed by Voldemort

Ptolemy - a wizard depicted on the Chocolate Frogs trading card series

Quirrell, Prof. - nervous, stuttering professor of Defense Against the Dark Arts

Ravenclaw, Rowena - One of the four founding wizards and witches of Hogwarts

Riddle, Tom - the father of Tom Marvolo Riddle

Riddle, Tom Marvolo - a young Lord Voldemort; born of a muggle father and a witch who died in childbirth

Rockwood, Augustus - a Death Eater as attested by Karkaroff in his trial

LORD
VOLDEMORT

Sinistra, Prof. - the teacher of Astronomy at Hogwarts. Her lessons are scheduled every Wednesday at midnight on top of the highest tower

Skeeter, Rita - a sensationalistic reporter who always seems to know the scoop at Hogwarts; an "animagus"

Slytherin, Salazer - the founder of Slytherin House, he was a parseltongue

Snape, Severus - the Hogwarts Potions teacher, wants to teach Defense Against the Dark Arts, leader of Slytherin House

Sprout, Prof. - the professor of Herbology (plants) at Hogwarts and the head of the Hufflepuff house

Travers Mulciber - a Death Eater (Dark Wizard) as attested by Karkaroff in his trial

Trelawney, Sybil - the Divinations professor at Hogwarts; obsessed with prediction of Danger and death

Timms, Agatha - a witch with an eel farm who bets on the Quidditch World Cup

Vector, Prof. - the Arithmancy teacher at Hogwarts

Voldemort - the powerful Dark Wizard whom most refer to as "You-know-who". When Harry was a baby Voldemort killed Harry's parents and attempted to kill Harry, leaving a thunder-bolt scar on Harry's forehead

Warbeck, Celestina - the popular singing sorceress who appears on the Witching Hour radio program

Weasley, Arthur - Ron's father, works in the Misuse of Muggle Artifacts Department of the Ministry of Magic and enjoys tinkering with Muggle items

Wimple, Gilbert - member of the Committee on Experimental Charms, Ministry of Magic

Wendlin The Weird - a witch from medieval times who loved being burned; loved the Flame Freezing Charm; was burned forty-seven times in different disguises

Quidditch (P 67, 79 SS) - Is a sport which is as popular to Wizards as soccer and baseball are to the Muggles.

7 Team Players - Each team is comprised of 7 players that ride on broomsticks. The Goal Posts are located 50 feet in the air and the action takes place 10 feet to 120 feet in the air.

Players
  3 Chasers
  1 Keeper
  2 Beaters
  1 Seeker

Equipment
  1 *Quaffle* -   A ball that scores 10 points
  2 *Bludgers* - Heavy balls that try to knock players off their brooms
  1 *Golden Snitch* - The most important ball, the game ends when caught.

Scoring
     Quaffle through a hoop scores 10 points each time. When the Seeker catches the snitch, 150 points is added to the team score and the game immediately ends.

The Play - Each team has one Seeker. His job is to seek out the small, hard to find, Golden Snitch and capture it in his hand. The Golden Snitch is a bright gold ball with little fluttering silver wings and is extremely fast. The first Seeker to catch the snitch wins 150 points for his team and the game automatically ends.

While the Seeker is looking for the snitch, there are *two bludgers*, which are big, heavy balls that rocket around trying to knock the seekers off their brooms.   Each team has *two beaters*, equipped with large clubs. The *beaters* zoom after the *bludgers* trying to knock them into the opposing team players in addition to protecting against *bludgers* aimed at their seeker.

There are *3 chasers* that pass the *quaffle* to each other and try to put it through any one of the opponents 3 goals in order to score. Each team has a goal keeper that protects the goals.